MODEL RAILROADING IN SMALL SPACES

— SECOND EDITION —

Mat Chibbaro

KALMBACH BOOKS

DEDICATION

To my Mom, who never hesitated to drive me to all those hobby shops.

Kalmbach Media
21027 Crossroads Circle
Waukesha, Wisconsin 53186
www.Kalmbach.com/Books

Published in 2011
27 26 25 24 23 3 4 5 6 7

Manufactured in China

ISBN: 978-0-89024-772-3

All photos by the author unless otherwise noted.

Publisher's Cataloging-In-Publication Data

Chibbaro, Mat.
Model railroading in small spaces / by Mat Chibbaro. -- 2nd ed.

p. : ill. ; cm. -- (Model railroader books)

"Model railroader's how-to guide"--Cover.
ISBN: 978-0-89024-772-3

1. Railroads--Models--Design and construction. 2. Railroad tracks--Models--Design and construction. I. Title. II. Series: Model railroader books.

TF197 .C485 2011
625.1/9

Contents

1

INTRODUCTION

The space problem

Ideas for fitting ample scenery and operation into small areas

The author's daughter, Stephanie, operates the layout shown in Chapter 3. It is really two layouts in one: a home layout and club module. The layout rolls away on a flip-up base for quick and easy storage to save space.

Have you ever thought that you would like to have a model railroad layout, but that you had no space to build one or not enough space to do it right? This book will convince you that a respectable, detailed, and operable layout can take little or even no additional area from your home. All it takes is some creativity in locating and/or storing your layout, 1. With the innovative ideas in this book, space is no longer an excuse!

2 The author's son, Brian, rolls the Chapter 3 layout into a storage location, using the cradle described in Chapter 9.

3 The author's wife, Erna, enjoys the end table featured in Chapter 5. The complete, continuous-running layout takes no room at all, as it still serves its furniture function.

Many modelers find themselves living in a small house, apartment, or condominium, with only a small room (or portion of a room) available for a model railroad. You may even be living in a college dorm, military barracks, or mobile home.

Where does this leave so-called "armchair" modelers who want a place to see their daydreams become reality? Traditionally, these individuals could concentrate on collecting, making individual models, building dioramas, or simply planning a layout for a time when more space is available.

Some modelers join clubs that have permanent layouts. Modular layout groups have grown in popularity. Members of these groups have one or more modules (layout sections) that can be set up together at public shows to form a larger continuous-running layout. An example is Ntrak, a national organization that sets standards for N scale modules.

Clubs and modular groups are great ways to model or operate trains with little or no space taken up at home. But at home, many members of these groups either have no layout or only have individual modules. These modules usually don't have continuous running capabilities or enough switching features to make them interesting enough to operate by themselves.

Creative space solutions

Suppose that you want more than what traditional space-saving solutions offer. This book offers two ways to make that happen by using space creatively. One is creative layout storage methods and/or locations, **2**. The other is incorporating the layout in a piece of furniture, **3**. I also show how to provide an operable home layout within a module for club use.

My ideas have come about because of the space constraints in my own home and my will to overcome them. Being a woodworker as well as a modeler, I came up with many of the ideas featured in this book. Along the way, I incorporated space-saving concepts other modelers have used to solve their space problems. I boiled all of that information down to the layouts featured here, while emphasizing the use of simple tools and techniques and readily available materials. Anyone can duplicate these layouts, even with little or no woodworking experience.

Advantages and possibilities

The time involved in building a layout can be as (or more) enjoyable for some than operating it. This includes me. However, many people have busy schedules or multiple jobs. Small layouts take less time to build—as well as maintain. Don't forget that the larger the layout, the more time you will have to spend on tedious maintenance, such as cleaning track and wheels. Some modelers have dismantled larger lay-

4

A railcar makes the rounds of Freedonia as the city fire department tends to an early morning blaze. This highly detailed scene is on the compact layout described in Chapter 6.

5

Brian's 2' x 4' Ntrak layout "Cruisin' Weekend" is in the back seat of the author's compact vehicle on the way to a show.

outs in favor of smaller ones because of the maintenance required.

This does not mean a small layout must necessarily be a very simple one. You are much more inclined to make a layout highly detailed if it is small, both from the standpoint of time and the impact on your pocketbook. This is evident in many of the layouts featured in this book, especially the urban scenery, **4**, in Chapter 6. Large layouts can lack detail, making them less interesting to view. Even if your interests are operation-oriented, running trains is more fun in a nicely detailed setting.

Another advantage of small-space modeling is portability. This came to me as an afterthought, since I had no idea when I started the trolley layout many years ago that I would be bringing it to shows. All the layouts in this book will fit in a van, pickup, or sport utility vehicle. Some will fit in a car trunk or hatchback, **5**.

Portability also comes in handy at moving time—something families are facing now more frequently than ever. I recommend that all home layouts, regardless of size, be built in sections to allow them to be relocated at some point in the future, as household moves cannot always be planned or anticipated. Even if joints between sections are concealed with scenery, they can be disconnected, moved, and reconnected with relative ease.

Outdoor photography is easy with small layouts. Instead of relying on expensive photo lights, move that layout outside for some realistic sun.

Small layouts can be covered relatively easily—several methods of doing this are shown throughout the book. Covers provide many benefits. The track will rarely need cleaning because dust is kept out. Small fingers and paws are foiled very effectively, saving your layout from needless damage. Layouts are also much more presentable this way and can be located in rooms where many of your non-modeling guests can see your work.

Some may wonder if enough train operation is possible to keep their interest up in a small space. If switching (picking up and setting out cars) is your main interest, there is no question. Continuous running is entirely feasible, especially in N and Z scales. Dining tables have been made with continuous-running HO scale layouts. Narrow gauge also increases your possibilities by decreasing the minimum radius needed.

If you are a beginner, starting small is a practical approach. You will make mistakes, but they will be on a small scale on a small layout. Errors will be easier to fix and you are less likely to give up in frustration.

You can expand small layouts when more space becomes available. John Allen, one of the fathers of contemporary model railroading, incorporated an early 4' x 7' layout into his eventual basement-filling empire. Simply include turnouts that lead track "off layout" in the interim—such as the interchange track in one corner of the layout in Chapter 5. Another idea is to place an entire small layout—such as the trolley layout in Chapter 6—into a city scene in a larger layout.

There are many ways of making your layout seem bigger than it is. Bridges, tunnels, scenery view blocks, and mini-scenes all do this by breaking up the layout to the viewers and operators, **6**, **7**.

Two basic modeling concepts are important for small-space modelers. One is selective compression. This means decreasing the size of a feature to fit on a layout. Many prototype industries, for instance, would take up the space of an entire layout in this book if modeled in actual proportions. Our space limitations dictate that we reduce the size of our buildings and/or industries to fit the space available.

The other concept is "beyond the layout" thinking. One example is imagining that your layout is part of a larger rail system. Interchange tracks (imaginary connections to a larger rail system) and separate staging areas are examples. Another is an industry that is only partially modeled on the layout

Suggested tools

Required for all layouts

- Hand saw and miter box (or electric circular or saber saw)
- 3/8" drill (battery or electric)
- Twist drill bit set and countersink bit (or pilot bit)
- Sanding block or electric sander
- Claw hammer
- Nail set
- Needle-nose pliers
- Screwdrivers
- Measuring tape or yardstick
- Small putty knife
- Paintbrushes
- Hobby knife
- Tweezers
- NMRA standards gauge

Required for some layouts

- Soldering iron, solder, flux
- Wire strippers
- Flush cutting rail nippers (or motor tool with cutoff disk)
- Metal file
- Miniature drill (pin vise) and bits (nos. 61-80)
- Adjustable wrench or wrench set
- Hot glue gun (with low-temperature setting)
- Carpenter's square
- Clamps (various types)
- Craft pins

6

Details and humorous names such as these from a scene from the layout in Chapter 2 attract attention and maintain interest.

7

The visible scenery in this photo of one of the author's Ntrak modules only takes up about a square foot of space. The main thing to do is get out of your chair and get your hands dirty, even building a small scene with a some track, a few structures, and a little scenery.

to save space; the rest is presumed to be out of sight.

Making the best use of this book

All of these project layouts require no more woodworking ability or tools than would be needed for a more traditional layout's benchwork. A large or expensive tool collection is not required (see above). Most lumber suppliers will cut wood to size for little or no cost. For those with more tools or greater abilities, I illustrate some intermediate and advanced ideas in Chapter 9.

Each chapter builds on the previous chapter(s) to some extent. Modeling skills in earlier chapters are not repeated in later chapters. For example, basic scenery is shown in Chapter 1 and hill construction and rock coloring in Chapter 3. The first two chapters use sectional track, with flextrack for most of the later layout chapters. I indicate where you will need to refer back to other chapters.

I included a variety of eras, settings, and locations for the project layouts. Any of them could be set in a different era by simply changing the vehicles and rolling stock. To a smaller extent, signs and structures also date a layout. Remember that structures survive for many decades, or even centuries. Some modelers prefer to model specific prototype railroads, locales, eras, or even specific dates.

Mix and match ideas from the projects in this book to best serve your desires, abilities, or funds.

Challenge yourself, but be honest; don't bite off more than you can chew. If you get discouraged, you may leave this great hobby temporarily or permanently. The goal of this book is the opposite: to bring you into the excitement and camaraderie of active model railroading. Now let's get out of the armchair and have some fun.

1

2

When the layout is not being operated, the structures can be removed and the layout stored under a double bed.

CHAPTER ONE

The Raritan River Railroad

HO Scale Christmas tree layout that hides under a bed

This layout can be the centerpiece of a holiday display, and it can also be pulled out to operate any other time of year.

This first project layout will introduce you to many basic modeling skills, such as trackwork, road construction, simple scenery, and structure kits. All modelers start at this beginning level and improve their skills in the areas they enjoy, much the way this book is arranged. The track plan is as simple as they come. With two loops of track, it is meant for display running or operation on the main lines. The theme for the layout is a small-town USA main street scene. The structures are removable to facilitate the layout's storage under a bed (**1, 2**). The layout could, of course, be stored upright or flat in any other area large enough to fit it. A comparable plan in N scale would fit on a 24"-diameter base!

Track, wiring, and structures

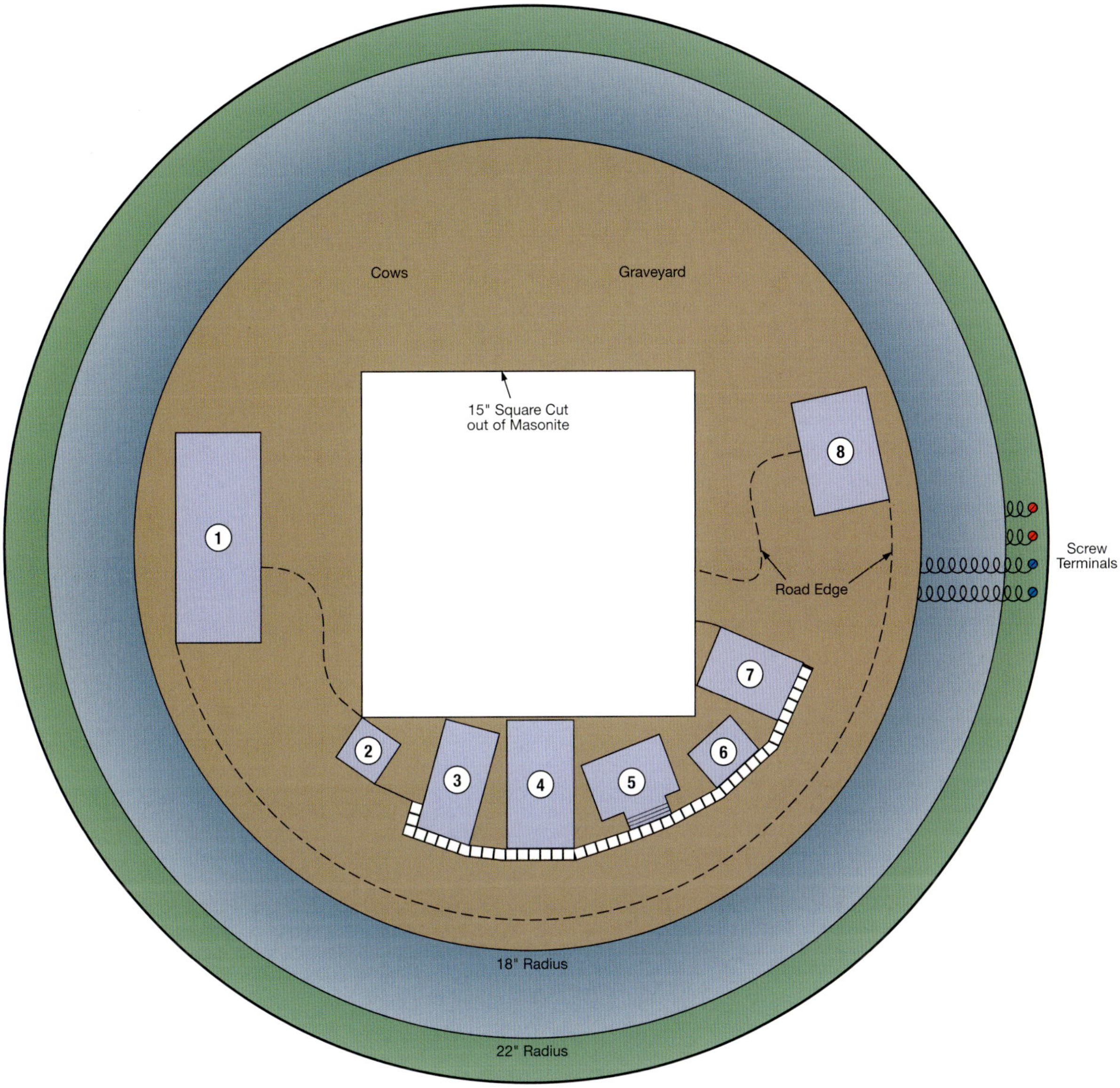

STRUCTURE	NAME	ORIGIN
1	Raritan River Freight Station	IHC #47785
2	Bobby's Garage	Model Power #483
3	Flo's Diner	Heljan #902
4	Slosher's Malt Shop	Heljan #902
5	Our Lady of Lourdes	Bachmann #45192
6	Garage	AHM #5835
7	Eureka Engine Co. 1	AHM #5835
8	Milltown Passenger Station	Atlas #706

4

3

A freight rumbles through town. All buildings are named after places in my hometown in the 1960s and 1970s.

Of course, this layout could be built with no center hole and be run without a holiday display. If it is to be used with a tree, use only an artificial one. Live trees require watering, and electricity does not mix with water.

Base construction

No room is needed under the layout for wiring, so it can be built directly on a plywood base, **4, 5**. Measure and mark both circles on the plywood. This can be done with a homemade trammel, **6**, or with a pencil and string wound around a nail at the center point. Base the radius of the inner circle on the size of your Christmas tree stand. I needed a hole 21½" across (10¾" radius) to clear the tips of the tree stand's feet. Use a saber saw to cut the plywood on the marked lines. Make a starter hole for the inner saw cut with a drill bit slightly larger than the blade.

Next, cut a piece of Homasote to serve as the subroadbed between the track and the plywood. Homasote is a cellulose-based sheet material that accepts track nails easily. I have not found it in sizes other than a full 4 x 8-foot sheet, but a 4 x 4-foot piece will be enough if you can find one.

Lay the plywood you just cut on the Homasote and use it as a template to mark the 48"-diameter outer circle. Make corresponding marks on the outer edges of both the plywood and the Homasote. This will help align them later, since your saw cuts will probably not be perfectly circular.

The inner cuts on the Homasote form a square that tightly fits around my tree stand (**4, 7**). You could cut the Homasote identically to the plywood; however you will then have less real estate on which to place structures. Buy your tree stand first and make any dimensional changes necessary to accommodate it.

Many modelers cut Homasote with a saber saw and a knife blade. This eliminates the mess caused by using a standard saw blade and results in a finished edge. However, the knife blade can be harder to keep on track. I prefer a fine wood blade, especially for free-hand cuts where you can't use a guide.

Plywood cutting diagram

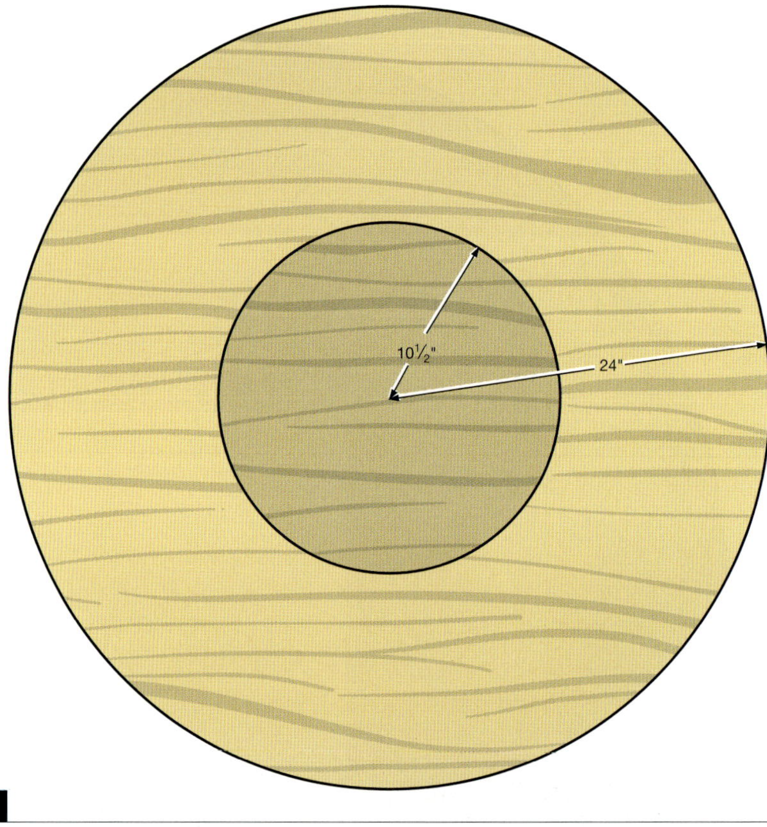

5

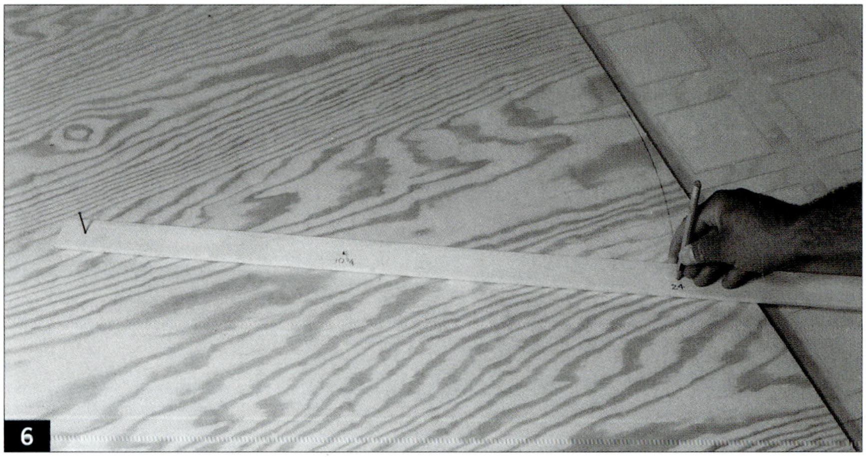

6

This homemade trammel is nothing more than a scrap piece of wood (a yardstick works well). Drill a hole for the nail at the center pivot point, and one for a pencil at each radius point.

Glue the Homasote sheet to the plywood with wood glue (**7**), adding weights to the top to ensure a tight bond. Sand smooth the edge of the assembly, especially on the bottom edge of the plywood, because the layout will have to slide along a carpeted floor. If you plan to slide this layout along a wood floor, consider a felt backing as shown under the work station in Chapter 8.

Track and wiring

The track for this project is sectional. This type of track comes in fixed lengths that fit together without having to be cut. The brand I chose also has integral roadbed; the ballast that holds the ties in place on prototype track is simulated by molded plastic fastened to the track sections.

Snap the sections together while lining up the rail joiners. Terminal

7

Place several weights on the Homasote/plywood assembly after gluing to obtain a good bond. You can see the square cutout in the center of the Homasote.

8

Here are the homemade power terminals. Far left: wire inserted into hole. Center left: screw turned into hole with wire. Right: alligator clips on screw terminals with wires leading to the power pack.

9

To install the track, grab a brad in the jaws of the needlenose pliers and start it into the Homasote. Push the brad in with the closed tip of the needle nose pliers until the head barely touches the ties.

10

Place the structures as desired, leaving room for the road and sidewalks. Cut and fit the sidewalk pieces, then mark all structure and sidewalk locations. Note the second layer of foam core under the church and the extra steps made from sidewalk scraps.

rerailer sections (with power wires) are available for the 18" radius curves. I ran wires to the outer loop by removing two of the supplied rail joiners and substituting Atlas terminal joiners. Run the wires in shallow trenches cut in the Homasote under both tracks to the outer edge of the Homasote.

Strip ½" of insulation from the end of each wire. Drill four 3⁄32"-diameter holes to a depth of ½" in the Homasote and use no. 8 x 1" sheet-metal screws for power terminals, **8**. Run the desired length of 22-gauge wire from the power pack to the alligator clips as shown. This will make it easy to disconnect the wires for storage or when moving the layout.

Before fastening the track to the base, finish drilling the 1⁄16" starter hole provided in the center of each track section. Then drive ¾" brads, **9**, through the holes to fasten each section down. Few, if any, adjustments should be necessary to the track, but test-run trains until you are sure there are no trouble spots.

Roads and scenery

Start by making road and structure bases from 3⁄16" foam core. This is polystyrene foam sandwiched between sheets of thin, smooth cardboard; it is available at arts and crafts stores. Cut it to fit inside the inner loop where the structures and roads will go. You will probably be able to overhang the Homasote a little, depending on your particular tree stand. Fasten the foam core to the base with wood glue.

Now take the sidewalks from the bases provided with the structure kits and piece them along the front of the center row of structures, leaving approximately 2" for the road, **10**. If you run out of sidewalks, more can be made as shown in Chapter 6. It obviously helps to have the structures

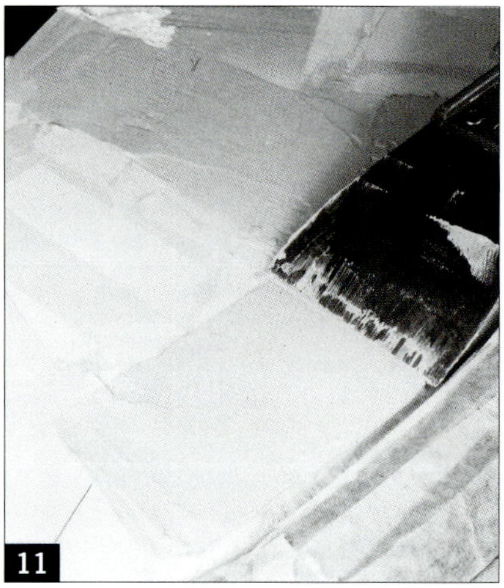

11 Apply joint compound to the street surfaces with a putty knife. Try to form a slight crown in the center—real roads have this to allow for drainage.

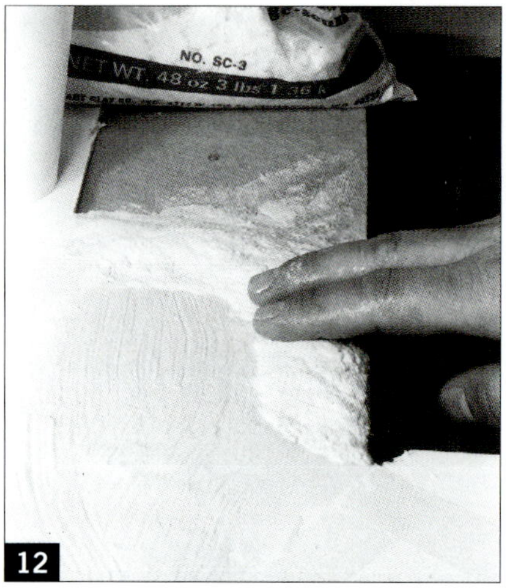

12 Still-wet Sculptamold can be shaped with any number of tools. For smoothing the surface, wet fingers are best.

13 After painting the roads, mask the structure bases and sidewalks. Use an inexpensive brush to apply beige paint for the initial application of ground cover.

14 Sprinkle the initial layer of ground foam or other scenery materials onto the wet paint. I like to use old spice or baby food jars with holes punched in the top. You can also see the folded piece of cardboard used to blow ground cover lightly into hard-to-reach areas.

15 Build up additional scenery layers and then bond them by spraying with a mix of matte medium and water.

done or close to completion for this step. Mark around all structures and sidewalks, and then remove them. Use masking tape to cover the locations of all sidewalks and structures, as well as the track and roadbed.

Cover road surfaces with joint compound. This is a plaster-based material used for drywall joints and is available at home centers or hardware stores. Use a putty knife to spread the joint compound, **11**. After about an hour of drying time, smooth the driest portions of the road with your fingers. Repeat this every 15 minutes or so until you get the texture you desire. Wet your fingers if the compound becomes too dry.

The other scenery material used on this layout is Sculptamold, a paper-based material available from crafts stores or hobby shops. It is easy to mix with water in small disposable cups. Use it to form small hills, **12,** and fill around the edges of the foam core. For a little additional relief, you could cut some shallow trenches in the Homasote with a utility knife to simulate dry creeks or gullies.

Sand the roads if they are too rough. Remove the tape from the sidewalk areas but leave it under the structure locations. Glue the sidewalks in place. Color the roads and the sidewalks with shades of gray craft paint, available in small bottles from various manufacturers in craft stores. When this dries, go back and tape over the sidewalks to protect them while scenery is done.

The easiest and most flexible scenery construction technique is the water-soluble method popularized by Dave Frary in the Kalmbach book *How to Build Realistic Model Railroad Scenery*. Brush a flat beige latex base color over all terrain around the roads and structure lines, **13.** While it's still wet, sprinkle on a layer of ground foam or real sifted dirt, **14.**

If you use real dirt as a ground cover, sift out the large lumps. Ensure there are no bits of ferrous metal lurk-

16 Paint all structure parts before assembly. The part closest to the ink bottle has been weathered with ink-alcohol solution. Good-quality water-based hobby paints are now available if you prefer them.

17 To simulate brick mortar, apply diluted white latex paint to the pre-painted wall sections and wipe off the excess.

18 For drybrushing, wipe most of the paint off the brush onto a paper towel, then drag the brush very lightly across the part. At left are various shades for a rust effect; at right, white highlights details.

19 Powdered chalk is a great way to simulate stains, rust, and dust. Wind-blown newspapers (reduced on a copier) are one method of hiding bad structure joints such as at the base of the chimney.

ing by passing a magnet through the dirt. This prevents locomotive magnets from gobbling them up later!

Continue layering different colors and textures, beginning with earth tones and finishing with grass colors, coarser textures, stones, and twigs. Spray the area liberally with matte medium solution, **15**. Matte medium is a clear adhesive and finishing product that dries flat (compared to white glue, which is slightly glossy). It's available at arts and crafts stores. Mix one part matte medium and four parts water, and add a few drops of dish detergent to help it penetrate. Woodland Scenics also sells scenery glue with a wetting agent. The company also sells flocking for even more realistic ground cover.

If you want to change the effect after the scenery is dry, simply layer on more materials and spray on more matte medium solution. It is almost impossible to make a mistake that cannot be hidden with a subsequent layer of scenery materials.

When you are done, remove all of the masking tape. Paint the edge of the plywood/Homasote base with the same flat beige paint used for the scenery.

Structures and details

All of the structures on this layout are made from easy-to-assemble plastic kits without structural modification. You can use the same ones listed in the bill of materials, or you can pick other ones to personalize your layout. In some cases the kits I used are no longer available; for those I list substitutes.

As you can see from the finished photos, it is possible to make these kits appear very realistic. This is fun and easy if you follow these painting and weathering tips:

1. Paint all structure parts with flat hobby paint, **16**.

2. On light-colored parts, use a mixture of 1 part India ink and 20 parts rubbing alcohol to darken crevices and provide a weatherbeaten look,

Begin by installing doors, windows, window glazing, and shades/ curtains onto the wall sections. Assemble the walls with liquid plastic cement to weld parts together.

Plant trees in the scenery base by poking holes with an awl or an appropriately sized nail. Notice the high level of detail in the alley and along the sidewalk.

Bill of materials

Lumber/hardware
- ½" plywood, 4' x 4' sheet
- ½" Homasote, 4' x 4' sheet
- No. 8 x 1½" sheet metal screws, 4
- * ¾" brads

Track and electrical
- 18" radius Bachmann E-Z Track, no. 44501, 3 pkgs.
- 18" terminal rerailer Bachmann E-Z Track, no. 44502
- 22" radius Bachman E-Z Track, no. 44503, 4 pkgs.
- Power pack, MRC Tech II Dual Power 2800
- Atlas terminal rail joiners, no. 842
- * 22-guage stranded wire, 2-conductor

Scenery
- Joint compound, 1 quart
- Sculptamold, three-pound bag
- * Woodland Scenics ground foam as desired
- * Matte medium
- Heki Mini Forest of trees, no. 302

Structures
- IHC no. 47785 freight station—substitute Cornerstone freight house, no. 3533
- AHM no. 5835 firehouse and garage—substitute Cornerstone fire station no. 3037
- Heljan no. 902 two stores
- Model Power no. 483 Bobby's Garage—substitute Bachmann no. 45174 gas station
- Atlas no. 706 passenger station
- Bachmann no. 45192 cathedral

Miscellaneous
- Tree stand
- * Wood primer
- * Flat beige latex paint, Sears no. 597 (or any other brand)
- * Gray craft paints
- * Wood glue
- 3/16" foam core board, 20" x 30" sheet
- * Masking tape

* Quantity as necessary or desired

16. One hint: Testor's and Floquil clear flat sprays are incompatible with the ink-alcohol mixture.

3. White latex paint diluted 1:1 with water simulates brick mortar, **17**.

4. Drybrush to streak on colors or highlight details, **18**.

5. Simulate the effects of rain and snow by brushing on diluted washes of a contrasting color.

6. Powdered chalks have a variety of weathering uses. Buy pastel chalk sticks from an arts or crafts supply store and rub them over some fine sandpaper, **19**. You can also buy them in powdered form in hobby shops.

7. Add detail parts to increase realism, especially on roofs—the most visible portions of model structures. Many detail parts can be fashioned from household materials to save money. Some can hide defects, **19**. Simulate vines by tracing lines with rubber cement or matte medium sprinkled with green ground foam.

8. Spray the inside of acetate used for windows with a clear flat spray such as Testor's Dullcote to simulate dust, screens, or wired glass (do this before installation). For a less-dirty but more see-though look, brush on Polly Scale Clear Flat Finish.

9. Make curtains or shades with colored paper or paint on the inside of the acetate. Place some details inside the windows of the structures if they will be viewed up close.

10. Follow the general rule of weathering a little at a time, regardless of the methods used. It is easier to add material than remove it.

11. During assembly, add paper view blocks in the buildings to limit the unrealistic see-through look. I often run a single piece of paper diagonally from corner to corner.

22

Both the railfan photographer at right and the crew member riding the diesel locomotive easing into the Milltown station had better be careful. This photo must have been taken in the days before OSHA.

Assemble structures on their own bases to keep them square, but don't glue the bases on, **20**. This gives you more flexibility in arranging the structures. Many bases are unrealistic, anyway. Place structures on the layout without glue so they can be removed before storing the layout.

Use powdered black chalk to weather the road. After applying the chalk, rub it with a dry finger. Remove any excess chalk with an ordinary pencil eraser. You can also use the side of an ordinary pencil to weather roads, followed by rubbing with a finger.

I planted commercially available trees in this chapter. Plant them as in **21**. I like to fix them in place with a product called Tacky Glue because it is very thick, although matte medium will also work. Larger trees can be removable if you omit the glue.

Figures and vehicles are a must for a complete, realistic scene. Trash, newspapers, animals, signs, benches, fire hydrants, trash cans, and similar details all add realism. Signs can be from magazines and brochures. Make sure that every detail and figure has a reason to be where you put it. Use cyanoacrylate adhesive (CA) to attach figures and full-strength matte medium for other items, **22**.

Any rolling stock can be used on these standard-radius curves. You can weather rolling stock as with buildings. It's easier if you remove trucks and couplers first. Diluted washes and powdered chalks work well. A clear flat spray will seal the weathering effects.

Layout variations

You can alter almost any aspect of the layout to suit your available space or other needs. Here are some possible variations:

- Make the layout without the center hole if not using a Christmas tree.
- Hang the layout on a wall with hooks or brackets when not in use.
- Kitbash structures (by modifying kits) or try scratchbuilding one or more of them.
- Replace one loop with a passing siding and stub-ended spurs.
- Make the base four feet square and add spurs in corners.
- Use a hollow-core door as a base for an HO switching layout or an N scale continuous running layout. This will slide easily under a bed. Install folding legs to set it up as a table instead of a Christmas tree display. (Legs are available from several sources, including Rockler Woodworking and Hardware—see the reference section.)

1

CHAPTER TWO

The Norwest Terminal

Building an HO scale cabinet-top switching layout

My daughter and son operate the Norwest Terminal, a small layout that can fit—temporarily or permanently—atop a bookcase or cabinet.

I've designed this HO scale layout, **1**, representing a port city's industrial area with operators in mind. The switching type of plan offers many possibilities in terms of sorting and spotting cars. A passing siding separates the layout into two areas: one with a small yard and engine facilities and the other containing industries to be serviced. The track plan is a modified version of plan 6 from the Kalmbach book *101 Track Plans for Model Railroaders*.

2

It's easy to store the layout upright in a closet. Leaving the backdrop in place protects the structures.

3

Engine No. 2 has just spotted an empty flatcar at the container yard.

Track and wiring diagram

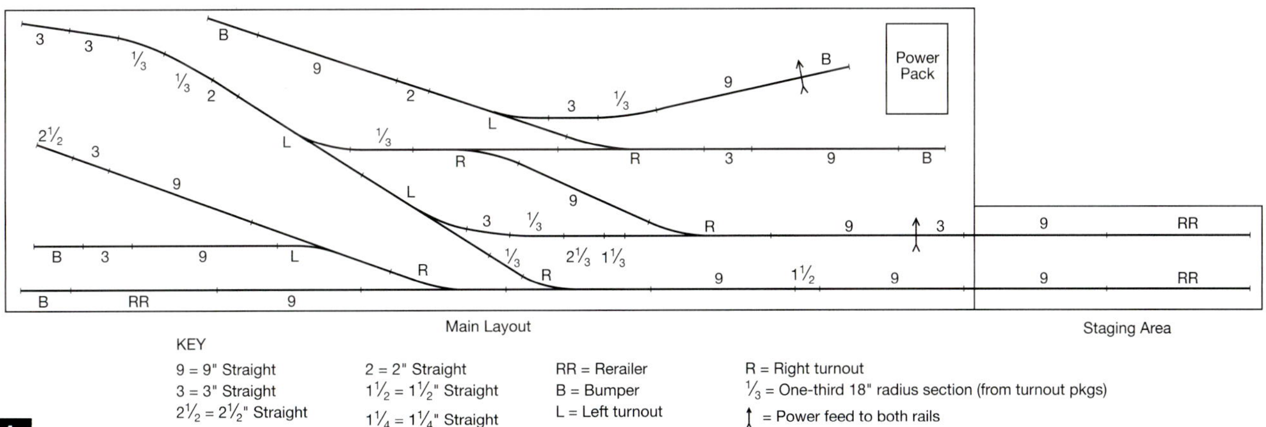

4

The plan also includes an optional separate staging area to allow trains to exchange rolling stock to or from the layout. You can think of it as a car ferry, and if you want, you could even model it to resemble one. The idea is to add operational possibilities that are more interesting than using your hand to rotate rolling stock directly on or off the layout. You could take this concept one step further and have receiving tracks set up at some remote destination (such as the other end of the car ferry route).

Most of the techniques used in this chapter are slightly more advanced than those in Chapter 1. The base is an open frame instead of plywood. Structures are more than unmodified kits, and a backdrop adds realism. I also lettered the locomotive, water tank, and container crane for the railroad.

This layout's size makes it conducive for storage in a closet. When upright it will fit below the standard hanger rod height, **2**. Here's another idea: most closets have one shelf above the hanger rod. If the closet is large enough, add a higher shelf and put that higher space to use. If you prefer, make the backdrop or the structures removable to fit where you want, **3**.

Frame construction

The frame material for this layout is no. 2 pine 1 x 2 boards. These are

Main layout frame

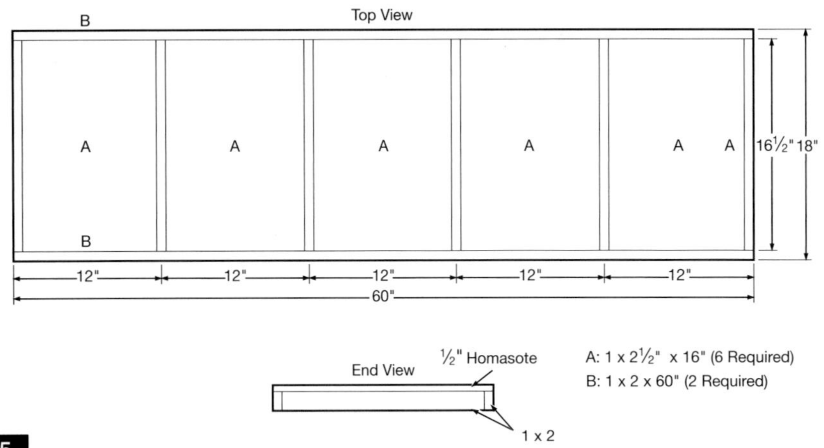

5

Staging frame, top view

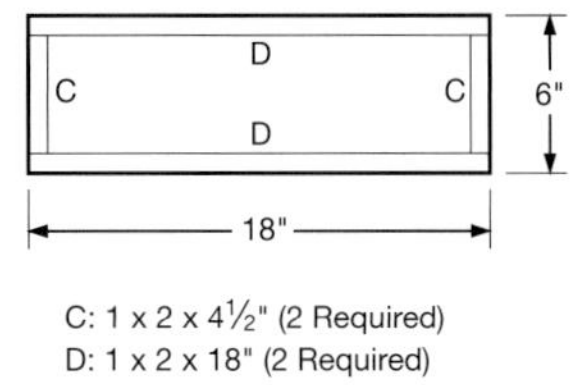

6

Cutting diagrams

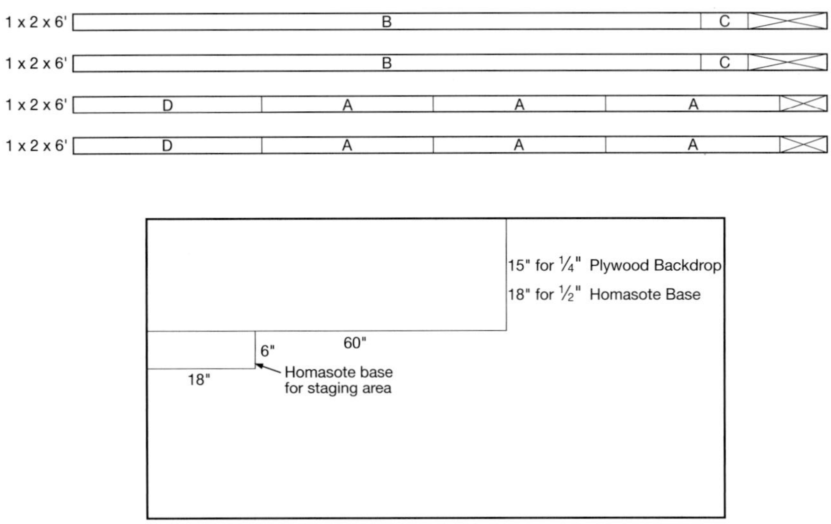

7

actually ¾" x 1½" in cross section (the nominal size comes from the boards' dimensions before they are planed and finished). This frame will elevate the track enough to allow wires to be run underneath, and it will also provide a good mounting surface for the backdrop (**4** to **7**).

Cut the 1 x 2s as shown in the diagrams with a hand saw and miter box, **8**, saber saw, or circular saw. Use nails and wood glue to fasten the pieces together, **9**. If you will paint the frame later, countersink the nail heads with a nail set, fill all holes with putty, and sand the areas smooth when dry.

Cut the Homasote subroadbed as outlined in Chapter 1. Fasten it to the frame with no. 8 x 1" flathead wood screws after drilling pilot holes, **10**.

Removable backdrop

A backdrop greatly increases the realism of a layout. Here you'll mount commercial backdrop scenes directly onto a piece of plywood. The seam between the backdrops will be mostly obscured by the elevated water tank later. To really set your layout in a specific place, you can mount actual poster-sized photo enlargements for backdrops.

Cut the ¼" plywood to the dimensions given, **11,** with a saber saw or circular saw. Cover all surfaces of the plywood with a wood primer.

Cut the backdrops to fit the plywood with a sharp hobby knife. Mount the backdrops to the smooth side of the plywood, **12**, using rubber cement. Spread the cement on the backdrop and the plywood (thin it slightly if it is too thick to brush on readily). When the cement is tacky, slowly and carefully position the backdrop in place and then press it with a roller (paint, kitchen, or wallpaper rollers will work). Rub off any excess cement with a rubber cement pick-up or a dried blob of rubber cement.

Use hanger bolts and wing nuts to mount the plywood backdrop if you want it to be easily removable. Alternatively, use roundhead wood screws for semi-permanent mounting.

Hanger bolts have threads like a wood screw on one end and machine threads on the other end to accept a nut. For the no. 10 x 24 hanger bolts, drill three ⅛" holes through the plywood backdrop and into the pine layout base. Enlarge the holes through the plywood only with a 7⁄32" bit. Install the bolts, **13**, then the backdrop and wing nuts, **14**.

When it's finished, remove the backdrop assembly to avoid damage while you install the track and add the scenery. When the layout is completed, I recommend leaving the backdrop in place as much as possible to avoid damage to the taller structures.

Track and wiring

The track used for this layout is sectional. Mount it directly on the Homasote subroadbed with no road-

8

It's easy to cut frame members to length using a hand saw and miter box. A power miter saw also makes quick work of the job.

9

Place the frame members on a flat surface for assembly with nails or screws and glue.

10

Use screws to fasten the Homasote to the frame. The pilot bit in the drill makes the appropriate-sized bore and also countersinks the hole for the flathead screw all in one operation. You could also drill and countersink the hole separately.

11

Clamp a straightedge to the plywood to guide the saber saw or circular saw. This cut could also be done with a handsaw, but it will take longer.

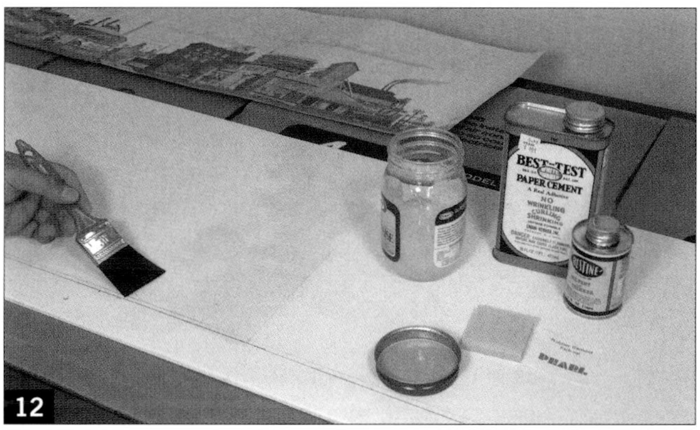

12

After priming the plywood for the backdrop, mark the backdrop locations on the plywood. The vertical line is the joint between the two backdrop scenes. The horizontal lines are the location of the top edge of the Homasote and a parallel line ¼" below it, so that the backdrop will sit lower. The rubber cement is being applied for the left side backdrop.

13

Install the hanger bolt by placing a pair of nuts on the machine threads and turning it with a wrench. Then remove the nuts.

14 **Install the backdrop by using a flat washer and wing nut for easy removal.**

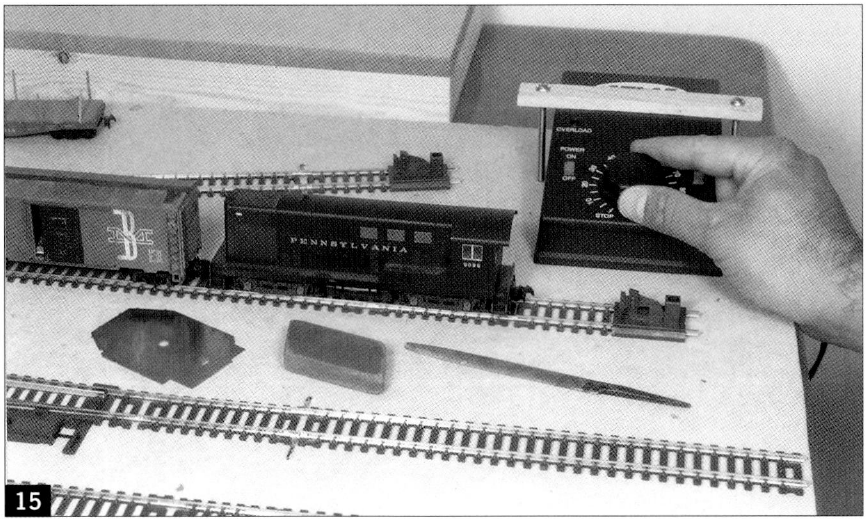

15 **Test-run trains after adding track, wiring, and the power pack. In the foreground, the tools for track troubleshooting include (left to right) an NMRA gauge, abrasive track cleaner, and file.**

16 **A better view of the NMRA standards gauge being used to check rail center lines.**

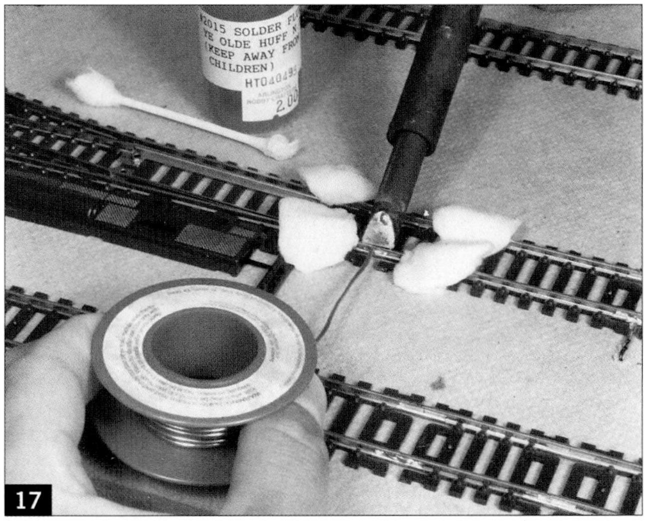

17 **When soldering a track joint, the wet cotton balls act as heat sinks. The liquid flux shown is easy to use and leaves no residue.**

18 **Design Preservation Models provides good instructions for assembly of their modular components. The Frank & Stein Fabricating Company main wall is shown under construction.**

bed. This better simulates real trackage in yard and industrial areas where the roadbed profile is relatively flat. If you prefer to include cork roadbed, refer to Chapter 3. The track components in the bill of materials have brown ties for better appearance without painting. You can also refer to Chapter 3 if you'd like to paint the track and ties.

Assemble all track in place as indicated in the track plan, **4**. Note that the ⅓-section 18"-radius sections are not included on the bill of materials because they are included with the turnouts. Also remember the two sets of terminal joiners—one set would suffice for a single-block layout, but the minimal extra effort now for redundancy may save a lot of work later. Feed

Norwest's brand-new GE 70-ton diesel switcher makes a runaround move to deliver a boxcar to a customer.

the power wires down through 3⁄32" holes drilled through the Homasote and then back up through holes drilled near the rear of the power pack. If you would like to divide the track into electrical blocks to have more than one locomotive on the layout at once, refer to Chapters 3 and 5.

After assembling all the track sections, use Atlas track spikes to hold them in place. This process is identical to the use of brads as shown back in Chapter 1 (photo **9**).

Start spiking down the passing siding in the middle and work outward in all directions. Continue spiking all sections of track. Make sure all joints are square and that all rail joiners are seated properly. If necessary, trim any gaps in the rail with a rail nipper as shown in the next chapter (**3-26**). Be sure to wear safety goggles. Lay the track on the removable staging area after butting it to the main layout on a flat surface (preferably where it will actually be used).

Mount the power pack directly onto the layout, **15**. I used a ¼" x ¾" x 5½" piece of pine (cut from a scrap 1 x 2) and 3" bolts with washers and nuts below the layout. You could also use a full piece of 1 x 2 and 3½" bolts or hook-and-loop fasteners (such as Velcro). Connect both power wires to the power pack track terminals.

Now test-run trains to ensure that the track is free of defects, **15**. The National Model Railroad Association (NMRA) track gauge, **16**, is a handy tool to detect problems with track, turnouts, and wheelsets. A file may be necessary to clean up any problems with the rail. Be sure to vacuum up all metal filings before getting any locomotives near the layout—remember that the magnets in their motors never lose their appetite for those filings!

Solder all track connections. If the layout will be exposed to a range of temperature and humidity conditions, leave a few track joints unsoldered to allow for rail expansion. If you need expansion gaps later, simply cut them with a small saw and, if necessary, feed additional power wires to the track.

If soldering seems intimidating, practice on some extra track sections. Follow these hints and you will be surprised how quick and easy it is:

• Tin the soldering iron or gun by filing off any residue, applying flux to the tip, heating the tool, and then applying solder to the tip.

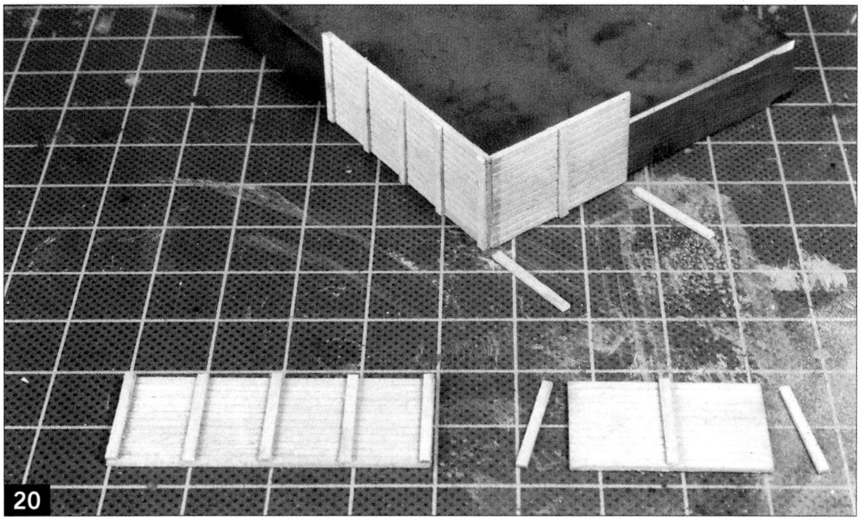

20

Use a 90-degree block to align adjoining bin walls for gluing. The other two walls and all four strips that cover the corner joints are on the cutting mat.

Structure locations

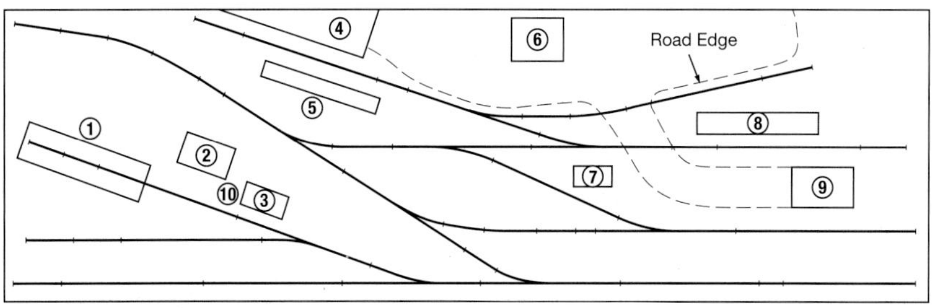

NO.	NAME	METHOD	ORIGIN
1	Engine Shed	Kit	Heljan #404
2	Crew Shack	Kit	Atlas #702
3	Sand Bin	Scratchbuilt	Basswood Parts
4	Frank & Stein Fabricators	Modular	Design Preservation Models
5	Central Gas	Kitbash	Walthers #933-3129
6	Norwest Water Tank	Kit	Korber #128
7	Gate Tower	Kit	Atlas #701
8	Leviathan Gas Tank	Kitbash	Walthers #933-3129
9	Leviathan Office	Kit	Walthers #933-3003
10	Fuel Column	Kit	Creative Model Assoc. #1002

21

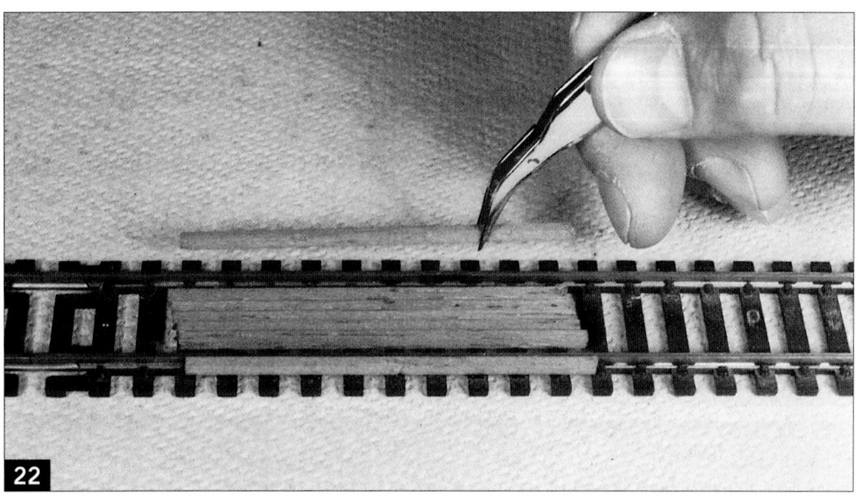

22

Make the grade crossing with stripwood.

• Use resin-core solder exclusively (never acid-core, as the joint will eventually corrode) and a compatible flux.

• Place wet cotton balls or fabric on either side of the track joint. This will help keep neighboring ties from melting.

• Apply flux to the joint with a cotton swab, or apply paste flux with a brush. This will help the solder flow into the joint.

• Unwind approximately 6" of solder.

• Heat the joint with the soldering iron held in one hand and the solder in the other, **17**.

• When the rail (*not* the iron) is hot enough to melt solder, apply enough solder with your other hand so that it flows through the entire joint. Apply solder from the outer side of the rails in case a solder blob forms.

• Remove the iron immediately to avoid melting ties.

• When the joint cools, file off any solder on the tops or insides of the rails.

• Rub an abrasive track cleaner (such as a Bright Boy) over the railheads. Vacuum up all filings and debris. Test-run trains over the joint and fix any bumps or bad spots.

Structures

In this project, you'll see some possibilities beyond building structures directly from kits. I kitbashed (modified) some and made a small building from scratch (raw materials). This can be a lot of fun and can really personalize your layout. I not only selectively compress the industries, I made only portions of some to save space.

Construct the large Frank and Stein Fabricators building from modular components made by Design Preservation Models. The company offers a wide variety of brick structure wall and detail components and templates to assemble a building of just about any size and configuration, **18**. With only three packages of components (lower floors, upper floors, and loading dock risers) and some sheet styrene for the roof and loading dock, I made a triangular-shaped partial building for one of the sidings, **19**.

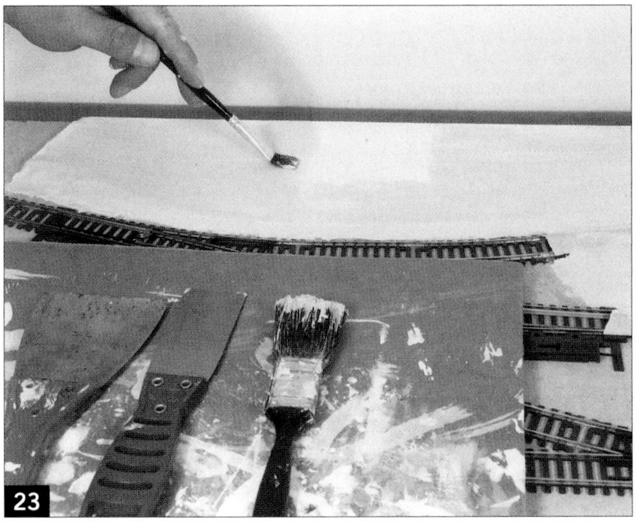

After applying joint compound to the road surface, smooth it as it dries with a finger and/or a soft brush. The tape over the tracks is omitted for clarity.

Glue each structure in place with a bead of full-strength matte medium around the base.

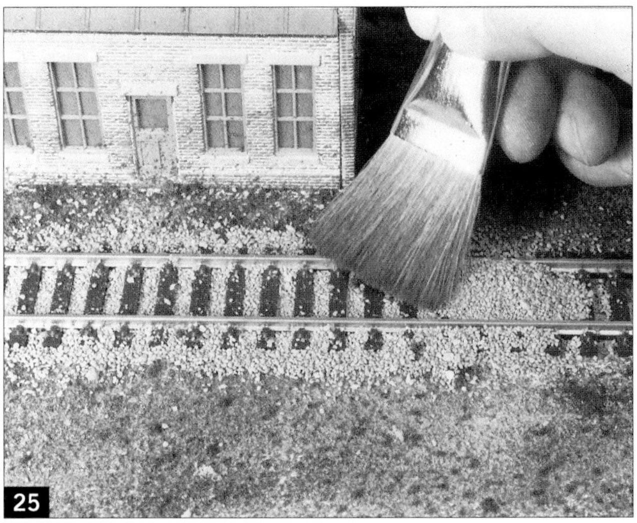

Spread ballast with a soft brush so that the ties are buried but the tops are uncovered. Work in small sections at a time.

After spraying the ballast with "wet water," bond it in place with matte medium solution.

The sand bin is an easy first scratchbuilding project. Buy the scribed sheetwood and stripwood listed from a hobby shop or online supplier. Cut two sides each, ¾" x 1¼" and ¾" x 2", from the scribed sheet. Weather these and the stripwood as you desire. Dirty paint thinner weathers wood realistically.

Cut the vertical braces from the stripwood, glue them to the sides, and then glue the sides together using wood glue, **20**. After installing the sand bin on the layout, place some sand in it and glue it with matte medium solution. Don't flood the bin with the solution or the wood joints may break. There you go—you've completed your first scratchbuilding project!

The two propane tanks on the layout are from the same kit. Modify them and use them for two separate industries. Simply paint them different colors and use different signs, **21**.

Letter the water tank to personalize the layout. I used Microscale decals meant for Norfolk & Western diesel locomotives. By rearranging the letters, I made the "NORWEST" lettering. You can come up with any name your imagination supplies.

To add depth and scenery, you can also add photo flats or low-relief buildings against the backdrop, such as the Radical Flats line from King Mill Enterprises (see the suppliers and manufacturers section).

Ballast and scenery

Make the grade crossings with stained lengths of $\frac{3}{16}$" square stripwood inside and outside the rails, **22**. Glue them with full-strength matte medium, leaving room for wheel flanges. When they're dry, sand or shave any strips that protrude above rail level and touch up the stain. Cover the track and grade crossings with masking tape and make the roads as Chapter 1 explains, **23**.

Install the structures, except for the engine shed, **24**. You'll install the engine shed after ballasting the track inside. Create some vertical relief in places by building terrain up with Sculptamold or by cutting down into the Homasote with a knife. Apply the

27 Tree materials include (back row) sedum for deciduous trees, goldenrod for evergreens, and unknown twigs for dead trees. In the foreground are bumpy chenille with a small evergreen cut from it and pine cones for small round trees.

28 Spray tree armatures and forms with ordinary hair spray to prepare for the application of ground foam.

29 Sift ground foam on the tree the same way you cover terrain. Use a few layers, spraying between each layer, and finishing with lighter colors for highlights. A plate below each color holds excess foam for reuse.

30 After painting the muscle of the Norwest Terminal, personalize it with decals.

31 Here's the staging area, showing the dowels that mate with the holes in the layout frame to ensure that the tracks align properly.

32 The locomotive pulls a covered hopper car from the staging area. This method beats adding and removing cars by hand.

initial layer of flat beige paint and ground foam texture except under the engine shed.

Pour the ballast onto the track approximately 2" at a time and spread it with a soft brush, **25**. Do the turnouts last and be very careful near the moving point rails and throw bar. Before starting, lubricate the turnouts with light plastic-compatible oil to help repel ballast cement that may inadvertently wick over to them.

Spray the ballast with wet water (water with a few drops of detergent or rubbing alcohol added) and flow matte medium solution gently onto the ballast from a dropper or dropper bottle, **26**. Old contact lens solution bottles work well for this. When the ballast is dry, move the turnout throw bars to ensure there are no problems.

Install the engine shed. Work the additional layers of ground cover right up to all the structures and into the ballast as you proceed. This will simulate poorly maintained industrial trackage. Normally, the ballast step comes after most or all ground cover installation.

Cover the bases of the structures but not the foundations. This will make the structures appear realistic. If any scenery material gets onto structures, brush it off with a stiff brush.

You can make some ground texture material yourself by grinding up dried leaves with some water in a blender. Spread the resulting mess out to air-dry. Important point: Be sure other blender users don't mind (be sure to clean all evidence thoroughly!). Finally, weather the road with powdered chalk or a pencil.

Bill of materials

Lumber
- 1 x 2, 8' No. 2 white pine, 4
- ¼" plywood, 4 x 8 sheet
- ½" Homasote, 4 x 8 sheet

Hardware
- Bright finishing nails, 1½" (4d)
- Flathead wood screws, No. 8 x 1", 12
- Hanger bolts, no. 10-24 (3), with washers and wing nuts
- Bolts, no. 10-24 x 3" (2) with washers and nuts

Track (Atlas)
- No. 2540 track nails, 1 pkg.
- No. 90860 LH manual turnout, 4
- No. 90861 RH manual turnout, 5
- No. 90821 9" straight, 2 pkgs.
- No. 90823 3" straight, 2 pkgs.
- No. 90843 bumpers, 3 pkgs.
- No. 90844 rerailer, 1 pkg.
- No. 90847 assortment, 1 pkg.

Electrical
- Atlas No. 310 power pack
- Atlas No. 842 terminal joiners, 2 pkgs.

Scenery
- Instant Horizons backdrop no. 711
- Instant Horizons backdrop no. 713
- Ballast, Woodland Scenics medium brown, no. B79
- Matte medium
- Ground foam (various)
- Joint compound
- Weeds for trees

Structures
- Walthers propane tanks, no. 933-3129—substitute Plastruct no. 1019 twin LP gas storage tanks
- Walthers Leviathon Mfg., no. 933-3003
- Atlas elevated gate tower, no. 701
- Atlas trackside shanty, no. 702
- Korber water tank, no. 128—substitute Walthers no. 2825
- Heljan engine shed, no. 404—substitute Model Power no. 553
- Creative Model Associates oil column, no. 1002
- DPM modular components, nos. 301-32, 301-08, 301-15 (1 each)
- Styrene sheet, .080"
- Scribed basswood sheet, 1/16"
- Stripwood, 1/16" x 1/32" (1 pkg.)

Miscellaneous
- Flat latex beige paint
- Semi-gloss latex beige paint
- Gray craft paint
- Wood glue
- Wood putty
- Microscale decal set no. 87-554
- 3/16" foam core, 16" x 20" sheet
- Basswood strips, 3/32" square, 2
- ¼" dowels, 2

Homemade trees

I believe that trees made from weeds are more realistic than many of the commercial models available, and I know they are cheaper. In the fall, go out and gather dried weeds that are the correct shapes for the trees you desire, **27**. One I find to be very useful for deciduous trees is sedum.

Many kinds of dried flowers from arts and crafts stores are suitable for tree armatures. Two examples are gypsophilia and baby's breath. Also, you can cut up a synthetic product called bumpy chenille to simulate small evergreen trees.

After trimming the tree armatures to suit your taste, spray them with inexpensive hair spray, **28**. Immediately sprinkle on various shades of ground foam, **29**. Begin with darker shades to add depth. When planting trees, keep in mind areas that you'll need to reach for uncoupling cars and for throwing turnouts.

Add whatever detail parts, figures, and vehicles you want. The container crane is also decaled "NW" for Norwest. Brush a coat of semi-gloss paint (I used beige) onto the outside of the main layout frame for a neater appearance.

Rolling stock and operation

The locomotives and rolling stock you can use is limited only by the size of the layout itself. A small switching-type locomotive works well and fits the theme of the layout. The GE 70-ton switcher I chose is from Bachmann.

I chose to paint and decal the locomotive to provide additional personality to the layout. This is by no means necessary. I used the same Norfolk & Western decals as the water tank earlier, **30**. Rearrange the letters, including turning over a "W" to make the "M" in

Just like any other crew, some members work harder than others.

"TERM." You can even create a custom logo on a computer and use blank decal paper to print it.

Rolling stock 40' long and shorter works the best because of the lengths of the passing siding, spurs, and lead tracks. Here is one good place to exercise your modeler's license. For example, a container yard would be served by long container flatcars or well cars. On the layout, you need to use shorter flatcars to simulate this traffic. I chose to model the manufacturing and fabricating companies because they would be served by a large variety of different freight cars.

I found that installing dowels to mate the staging area to the layout frame helps to keep the staging area in alignment while using it, **31, 32.**

It will help with switching if you weight your rolling stock consistently. This is more important than the actual weight you use. If you would like to follow the National Model Railroad Association guideline, it is 1 ounce per car plus ½ ounce per inch of car length (for HO scale).

Variations

Here are a few possible variations to this design:

• Mount a shelf or wall brackets on which to mount the layout as shown in Chapter 7. Use clamp lights on the backdrop for additional lighting.

• Mount another shelf above the layout, then mount lights below the upper shelf and use the top shelf for display.

• Staging can be pivoting (sector plate) or sliding (transverse). Both types are used frequently with display layouts in other countries and popularized here by the writing of Paul Dolkos and others in *Model Railroader* and *Model Railroad Planning*.

• Mount the layout on a fold-up, roll-away base as in Chapter 3.

• Arrange the layout to fold up like a hideaway (Murphy) bed. A foldaway mechanism to do this is sold by Rockler Woodworking and Hardware—see the appendix.

1

CHAPTER THREE

The Pacific Union Railroad

An Ntrak module/home layout with a fold-up, roll-away base

The Pacific Union module is at an Ntrak club setup connected to other modules to form a larger layout. It looks like the circus train has come to town. Phil and Janice Poole are in back of their module awaiting the start of the show.

This layout is really two in one. First, it is designed as an Ntrak module. Ntrak is a national organization that sets specifications for N scale layout modules of varying lengths and configurations. These individual modules are connected to form large layouts at public shows or club meets, **1**. The locations of the three common tracks that run among all modules are fixed at the module interfaces. The remainder of the module, including any private trackage, is left to the builder's discretion. This 2 x 4-foot module is the most common size built, affectionately known as a "plain old four-footer," or "POFF."

2

At home, the module does double-duty as a complete home layout. My wife is rolling the layout into a closet for storage, using the rolling base.

I added continuous-running private trackage behind the three shared tracks. This provides a complete, operable home layout between group setups. The photo on page 4 shows the module set up by itself. In addition, the private trackage is mounted on a removable lift-out section. This allows you to interchange scenes without having to build another module frame. It also allows display of the removable section in the coffee table in Chapter 4.

Ntrak publishes a module manual (available online free of charge at www.ntrak.org) showing all the information needed to build a basic module. This layout's design follows Ntrak's specifications for track and construction, but the suggested module top is replaced by two lightweight assemblies of foam and thin plywood—one part fixed, for the three shared tracks, and the other part removable, for the lift-out section.

Following my Ntrak club's policy, I installed the optional Ntrak wiring with power pole connectors instead of the traditional "cinch-jones" connectors. Both are illustrated in the Ntrak module manual.

In addition to the four removable legs necessary for Ntrak meets, you can make an optional rolling base for easy home storage. The rolling base will allow you to quickly and easily fold the layout up and roll it into a closet or other room, **2**. Remember to either remove the lift-out section or fasten it in place *before* folding the layout!

This layout also provides an introduction to inclined track grades and flextrack. Ntrak standards require flextrack for the shared trackage. Another advantage of flextrack is its ability to form tighter-than-traditional radius curves to incorporate the continuous-running private trackage within the standard POFF size.

Scenery becomes more three-dimensional. I'll demonstrate in this chapter how to build and color hills

3

The Santa Fe *Super Chief* rumbles through town while a pair of freight trains deliver cars to customers.

Track, structure, and wiring diagram

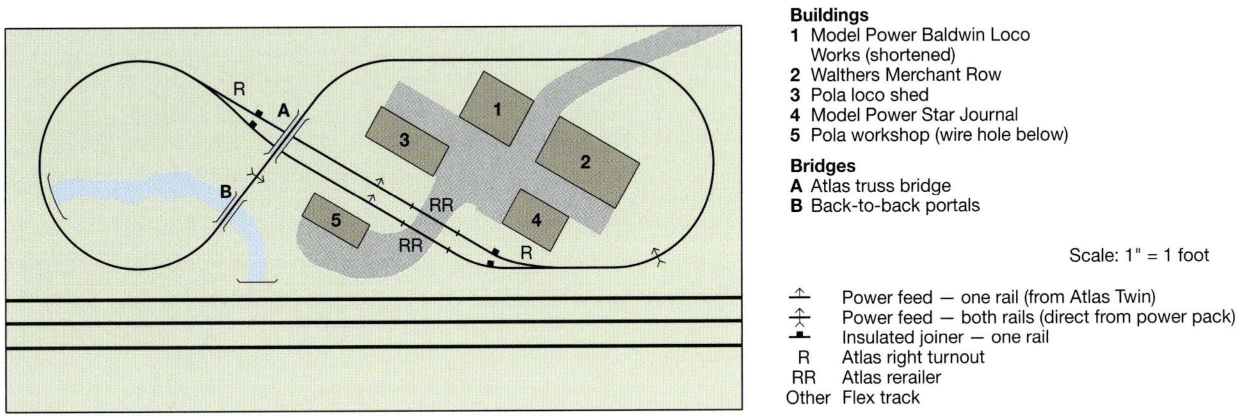

4

and rockwork from foam—the rigid extruded type used for insulation, not the beaded type you find more in packaging, **3**.

Frame, legs, and control box

Build the module frame much like the one in Chapter 2, but with 1 x 4 lumber per Ntrak specifications. This size consistency allows the modules to be clamped together (**4, 5, 6**). Cut members A and B. Use wood glue and 1¼" drywall screws in pre-drilled holes to fasten members A to B. (You can substitute flathead wood screws if you wish, but drywall screws have become popular for woodworking—they are inexpensive, drive easily, and hold well.) Countersink the screw heads, **7**.

Cut 1 x 2 cross members C and D as well as ¼" plywood member F and a piece of 1"-thick foam the same size as the plywood. Measure the combined thickness of the foam and plywood and mount cross-members C and D the same distance down from the top of the 1 x 4 frame, **8**. Before installing members D, check the clearance between members D and A for the legs.

Fasten plywood member F to cross-members C and D with wood glue and 1¼" drywall or wood screws. Mark the sides of member C where these screws are installed; you will see why later when the control box is installed. The module frame should now be very stable and yet lightweight.

Glue the foam you just cut onto the plywood with construction adhe-

Layout frame

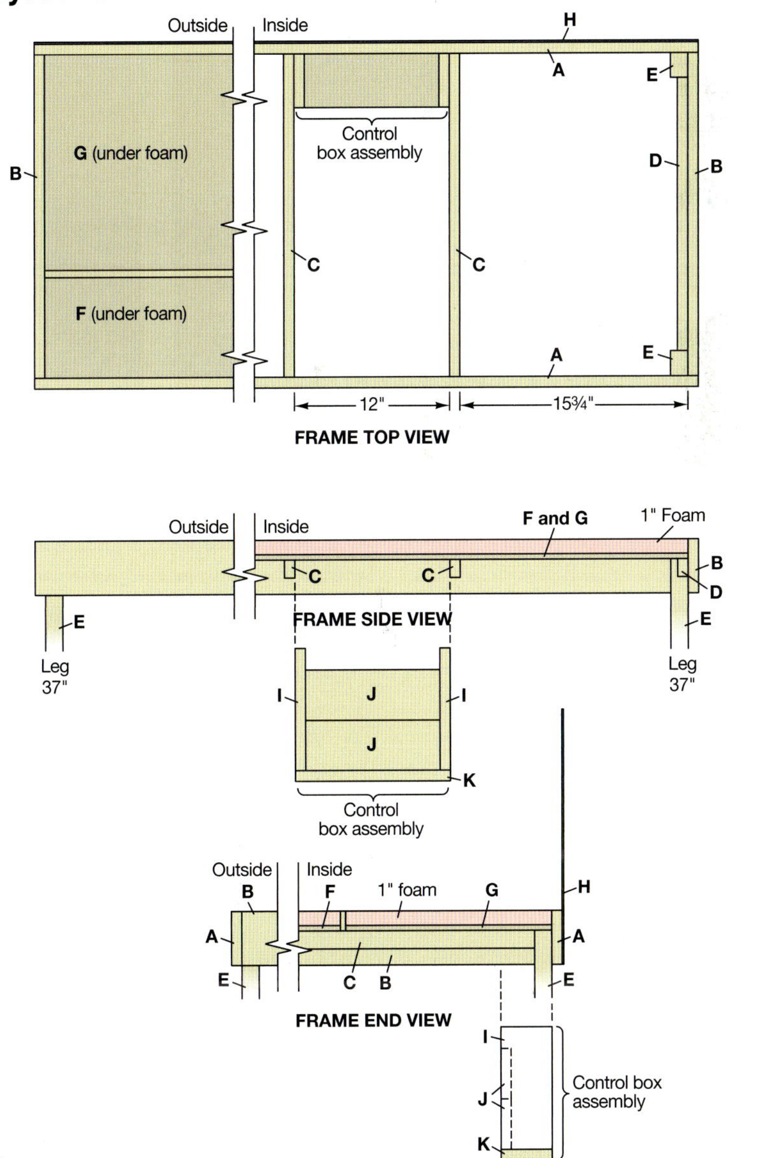

5

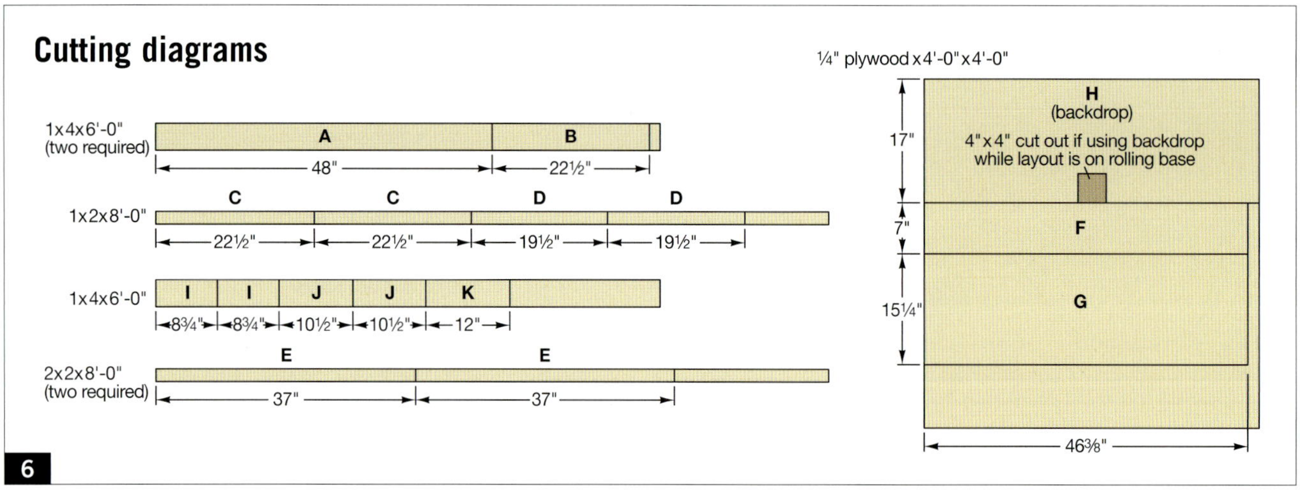

Assemble the outer frame members with drywall screws after drilling and countersinking pilot holes.

Install the frame cross members approximately 1¼" below the tops to leave room for the plywood and foam.

sive that is compatible for use with foam (read the label to be sure), **9**. If you don't have a caulking gun, buy the caulk in squeeze tubes. Weight the foam until it dries, which can take a few days. You can also use 1¼" drywall screws to hold the foam. Recess the screws slightly below the surface of the foam, then fill the gap between the foam and the frame with construction adhesive, **10**.

Cut plywood member G for the lift-out section, along with a matching section of 1" foam. Test-fit them to be sure they are easily removable. Glue these together without fastening them to the frame, **10**. After the glue dries, cut the access hole for the wire connector at the future location of a structure that will later conceal the connector.

Cut the Ntrak legs from 2 x 2 lumber to a length of 37". This will give you a track height of 40" from the floor when leg adjustment bolts are at their mid-adjustment point, per Ntrak specifications. Drill through the leg and frame for the 3" mounting bolts, **11**. Mark each leg's position in the base as you go to avoid confusion later.

Remove the legs and install the height adjustment bolts on the bottom of each. Drill a ⅜" hole approximately 3" deep into the end of each leg to accept a tee nut for the ¼" x 3" carriage bolt foot. Drill these holes as perpendicular to the leg as possible. The tee nut instructions call for a 5⁄16" hole, but a ⅜" hole allows more clearance for the bolt. Make sure the tee nut is centered in the hole, **12**. Note that the tee nuts are secured with additional no. 6 x ½" sheet-metal screws.

If you build the coffee table shown in Chapter 4 and use its drawer for controls, you will not need a control box. To build a box for the power pack, cut members I, J, and K. Fasten members I to members J (two each). Then fasten member K to the assembly, **13**, to complete the box. Drill mounting holes through the box and the frame cross members, **14**, to accept the ¼" x 2" flathead bolts, washers, and wing nuts. Drill these holes to miss the screws holding plywood F to member C (this is why you marked those locations earlier).

You may drill mounting holes at both the rear of the module (so you can access controls from inside an Ntrak layout during setup) and at the front of the module (if you would like to access controls while running at home and viewing the layout). The 2" bolts allow easy removal of the control box for storage or transport.

9

After securing the plywood for the fixed section to the frame, spread construction adhesive to secure the foam (which is being held in the background).

10

Once the fixed foam has been secured with screws, fill gaps with construction adhesive. In the background is the removable lift-out section being weighted down while the construction adhesive dries.

11

The frame is upside-down with the foam and plywood in place. Clamp a leg to the frame and drill the hole for its mounting bolts. After this, countersink the hole on the outside of the frame. The flathead bolt, washer, and wing nut that hold the leg in place are shown.

12

Add levelers to the legs. Start by (from left to right) drilling a hole in the end, adding the tee nut, securing the tee nut with sheet metal screws, and turning the carriage bolt into the tee nut.

Rolling base

The rolling base is optional, but it's a creative way to quickly fold and unfold the layout for quick conversion between storage and use at home, **15**. If you are happy using the four removable legs both at home and at Ntrak setups, feel free to skip this section.

Cut members L, N, and M from 2 x 4s. Fasten members L to M and attach members N to M using wood glue and no. 8 x 2½" deck screws. These screws are made to go in easier and faster than traditional wood screws; you may use either. Drill 7/64" holes to accept them and countersink the holes.

To strengthen the joints in the base, add gussets made from ¼" plywood (members O and P). Drill 7/64" holes through the gussets and into the 2 x 4 members. Fasten these gussets with no. 8 x ¾" roundhead wood or sheet-metal screws, **16**.

Now turn the assembly over and support it while installing the casters. I used no. 10 x 1" roundhead wood screws and washers for this. Check the size of the holes in your casters prior to purchasing these fasteners. If you cannot find suitable casters locally, they can be ordered from Rockler Woodworking or Constantine's (see the suppliers and manufacturers section).

Drill the ¼" mounting hole through both the layout frame and the rolling base, **17**. Install ¼" x 3" roundhead bolts with washers and wing nuts to allow the layout to pivot on the base. Flat washers are used at the head of the bolt, at the wing nut end, and between the layout and base. For stability, place the layout on its Ntrak legs for the remainder of its construction.

Removable backdrop

Make the plywood backdrop (or sky board, as it is called in the Ntrak manual) from ¼" plywood as shown in Chapter 2. Cut member H and drill three 3/16" holes through it and the

13

Assemble the control box with glue and screws. It will hold the power pack for operating the private trackage on the module.

14

With the frame upside down, clamp the control box flush with the top of the cross members. Drill ¼" holes for the flathead bolt. The countersink bit shown will recess the bolt's flat head.

Rolling base frame and cutting diagram

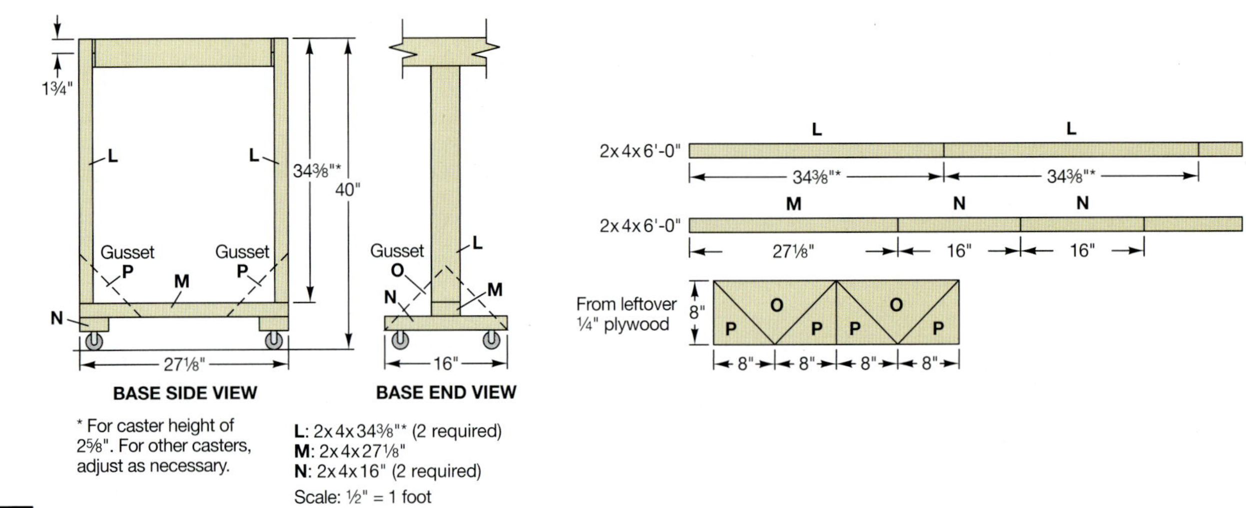

15

layout frame to accept no. 10 x 1½" roundhead bolts, washers, and wing nuts. Mount the backdrop with the screw heads facing the outside of the layout, **18**. This will prevent you from snagging operators at Ntrak setups—a quick way to become an unpopular club member.

I mounted the poster backdrop onto the plywood with spray adhesive. The source of the poster I used is unknown, but the appendix lists two online sources for posters and backgrounds.

Roadbed

Mark the locations of all track. Measure the exact distances of the three Ntrak lines from the front of the module. This is vital to ensure that the track will align with other modules. Use a straightedge to draw the center lines of these three tracks.

For the private trackage, it is difficult to use a compass to mark on the foam. Also, mistakes made marking the foam are hard to change. Because of this, I first drew the plan full-size on paper. Tape the paper onto the lift-out section and, with a pencil, poke through the paper along the track center lines to mark the foam, **19**. Remove the paper, connect the pencil marks with a permanent marker, and you have your track center lines.

I felt that easements would be beneficial with these tight curves. An easement is a gradual increase in the radius at the end of a curve that "eases" trains into the curve and helps prevent derailments. This can be readily accomplished by offsetting straight sections from the curve radius by ⅛", **19**. The flextrack flows from the curve into the straight section, providing an acceptable easement; this is much simpler and faster than figuring out the exact easement dimensions using formulas.

It was easy to make the grade on the private track with Woodland Scenics flexible foam inclines—I used the 4 percent grade. My preferred fastening

When all of the 2 x 4 rolling base frame members have been assembled, add plywood gussets for strength. In the foreground is one of the casters ready for installation.

After assembling the entire rolling base frame, place it and the layout frame upside down on a flat surface. Drill the holes for the pivot bolts through the base frame and the layout frame. The casters have been installed.

Removable bolts, washers, and wing nuts hold the plywood backdrop in place.

Mark track center lines with a pencil through the paper track plan and into the foam. At right you can see the ⅛" easement offset. The Ntrak main center lines have been drawn with a permanent marker.

method for these is hot glue, **20**. This goes quickly, but to avoid melting the foam, use a low-temperature glue gun or one with a low-temp setting. An alternative is construction adhesive, which requires pins or weights to hold the foam until the glue dries.

Follow the track center line as you go—the center lines can be seen through the zig-zag shape of the inclines. Glue about 4" to 6" at a time. If you break the incline, no problem—just continue gluing with the broken edges mated, **20**.

Since I wanted the passing siding to be flat, I began the incline just beyond the turnout under the center bridge. Each piece of incline raises the track 1", so you must then add a 1" foam piece under the next section of incline to get the proper height, **21**. Use the paper track plan to transfer the shape of the areas needing the 1" foam under the second level of inclines, and then again to transfer the track center lines once these pieces of 1" foam are installed. Continue the left-side incline up to the bridge area. Once again, transfer the track center lines to the top of the second-level incline—this time by sighting through the zig-zag incline pattern.

Repeat this process on the right side of the track plan, beginning beyond the other turnout. Plan ahead so that the inclines end up at the same height on the opposite ends of the center truss bridge. The resulting clearance under the bridge is slightly less that the NMRA standards gauge calls for. This was OK with me, as I wasn't planning to run any tall rolling stock anyway.

I installed cork roadbed on this layout. Begin adding cork at the diverging portions of turnouts, **22**. I like to use hot glue for this as well. Finish the turnout areas by piecing in the inner sections, **23**. Continue until all track

20

Hot-glue the first-level incline with Woodland Scenics flexible foam.

21

The second-level incline is placed on 1"-thick foam.

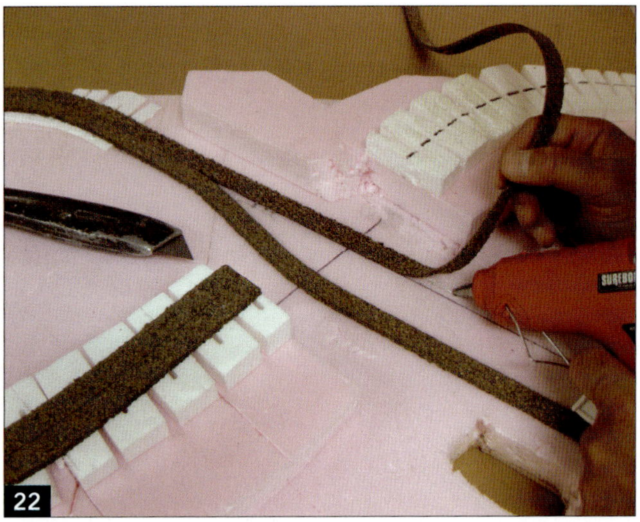

22

Install cork roadbed on the outer diverging sides of turnouts first. Cut the cork with a utility knife.

23

Cut sections of roadbed to fit in the middle sections of turnouts. The fit doesn't have to be precise.

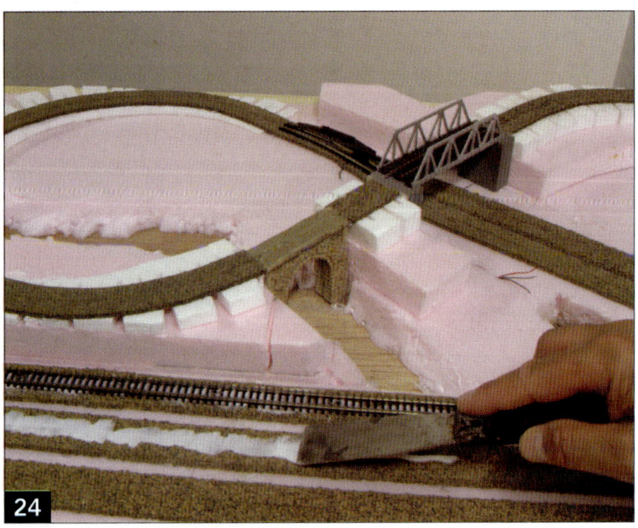

24

Spread a bead of construction adhesive along the middle of the roadbed with a putty knife. I have begun to cut the foam away for the river. This is also a good view of the bridges; both have been painted before installation.

25

Hold the track in place with pins while the adhesive is drying. Use a straightedge to ensure that the Ntrak main lines are straight. In the foreground are an unmodified 1¾" craft pin (on the left) and one that I cut down to 1" (right).

26

I prefer rail nippers for cutting flexttrack. You can also use a motor tool with cut-off disk. In either case, wear goggles! Here I have held the track in place temporarily while I cut it to fit the rerailer (next to the roadbed). You can also see the metal rail connectors and the cut-off ties waiting to be reused under the rail joints.

27

Solder the rail joint between the turnout and the curve while the flextrack is straight. This results in a smooth joint after the flextrack is curved. I purposely located the insulated joiners on the inside of the curve and the metal one on the outside for stability.

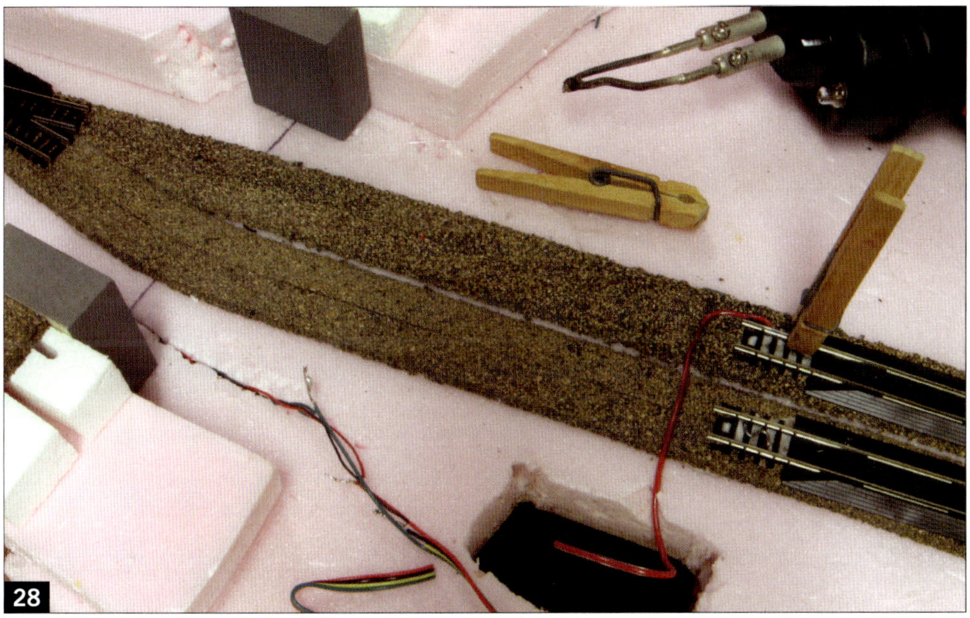

28

On the other side of rerailers, as I continue laying track into the passing siding, I have soldered one of the feeder wires to the track. The cotton balls have been removed for clarity. A pointed clothespin is holding the wire in place for soldering. Next to the roadbed is another clothespin –you can see how I sanded it to a point to do this job. Soldering clamps can also be purchased to perform this job. Notice the red feeder wire running through a trench cut in the roadbed and the foam, as well as extensions soldered to the turnout wire to reach the connector, which will extend through the hole.

sections are done. Sand the top of all the roadbed flat with a sanding block to eliminate any irregularities.

Cut the roadbed, incline material, and foam out from under the center truss bridge to allow installation of the bridge abutments. For abutments, cut blocks the correct height from scrap 1 x 2. Paint these with concrete-color craft paint, weather as desired, and glue them under each end of the future bridge location. You could also substitute commercial bridge abutments.

The track also needs to cross the creek. Another Atlas bridge could be used here, since the track is straight. For added interest, I created a stone arch bridge by gluing two single-track tunnel portals together, back-to-back. Sand the top to match the incline, paint, and weather them. After cutting out the correct amount of roadbed, incline material, and foam, install the portal assembly with hot glue, **24**.

Track and wiring

Flextrack can be bent and cut to fit as desired. The radius of the continuous-running oval is tighter than standard sectional track, which was necessary to fit the loop onto a standard module. Both turnouts are Atlas remote-control type. This allows you to throw the turnouts remotely from the operator's area inside the layout at Ntrak setups, or from outside of the table if you make the coffee table in Chapter 4.

We will divide the track into electrically separated track sections. This will allow you to hold a train on either side of the passing siding while you operate on the other. Place insulated rail joiners where shown in the track plan, **4**. Insulated joiners are made of plastic and therefore block current from pass-

29 **Continuing around curves, solder joints with the section straight, then bend the track into position.**

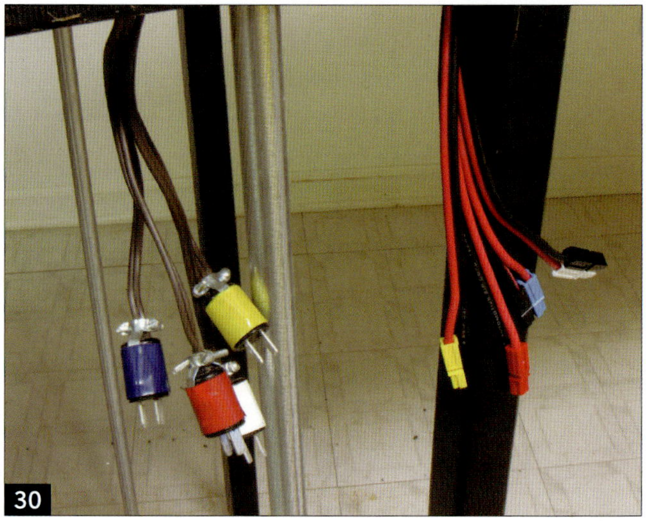

30 **The PU module is at right, with power pole connectors. The author's son's module (which also has a lift-out scenery section) on the left has traditional cinch-jones connectors.**

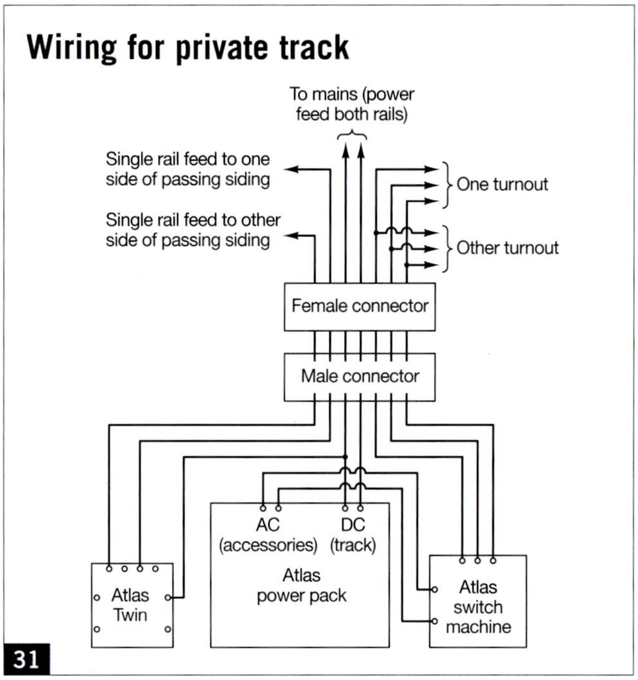

31

32 **Here's the control box with (left to right) the Atlas Twin, the power pack, and the switch machine controller. The female end of the nine-pin connector is hanging off to the right. The male end of the connector can be seen in 35.**

ing through a rail connection. They are only needed on one rail at each point on this layout, but make sure they are on the same rail at each location.

I began laying track with the Ntrak main lines. Since foam doesn't grip track nails like Homasote does (Chapters 1 and 2), glue the track to the roadbed with construction adhesive.

Spread a bead of glue along the roadbed in short sections (8"-10") and then smooth it into a thin layer, **24**. If the adhesive is too thick, it will ooze up between the ties when it's pressed into place. You will get the hang of it quickly, but consider practicing on some scrap track first.

Hold the track down with craft pins, **25**. These pins come in different varieties—some are T-shaped. The ones I used each have an S-shaped head with two 1¾"-long legs. I cut down some of the pin legs to 1" to use on the lower portions of the track. Be sure that you place them so that the rails are not forced out of alignment.

On the private trackage, start laying track at the turnouts and fit it in along the cork roadbed. Cut the rail slightly longer than necessary for each section. You can use a cutoff disk in a motor tool or track nippers that are specifically designed to provide a flush cut edge, **26**. Then, if necessary, use a file or rail cutters to trim the rail to the exact length needed and clear off any burrs.

Solder each rail joint (except those with insulated joiners) as explained in chapter 2. Photo **27** shows the turnout where I began soldering track. Notice that I placed the insulated rail joiner on what will be the inside of the curve. I soldered the metal joiner on the other rail while the flextrack was straight. This provides a smooth joint when

The steps to painted track: unpainted track (left), the rails and ties painted a dark brown (middle), and the rail sides highlighted with various rusty colors (right).

The module's scenery and structures make it look larger than it actually is.

the track is curved into position. Work slowly and carefully, and avoid forcing anything into place.

If you are not making the coffee table layout in Chapter 4, you can wait until all the track is done, solder feeder wires to the rails, and pass the wiring through holes in the foam/plywood assembly. I ran all wiring in trenches or slots cut into the top surface of the foam and through the roadbed leading to the hole for the connector, **28.** I ran these wires, extended the turnout wires, and soldered the track feeders to the outsides of the rails.

As you continue installing track, you will have gaps where ties were removed to install rail joiners. Fill these in as you go with scrap pieces of ties (after removing the molded-in spikes). The scraps can sit right on the same smoothed bead of construction adhesive that holds the track down.

Continue around the layout, bending the flextrack partway around curves, pinning it into position temporarily, and then soldering each succeeding joint with the flextrack straight at that point, **29.** This results in smooth curves when the track is bent.

Since this is two layouts in one, it requires two different wiring schemes. The wiring necessary for Ntrak setups is shown in the Ntrak module manual described in the beginning of this chapter. Follow the manual's

Here's an overall view of the foam built up for the mountains, the river cut-out, and the foam core road and structure base.

Carve away foam to form rock faces using a chisel. This can also be done with a screwdriver putty knife, or other tools. The track is taped to protect it from stray scenery materials.

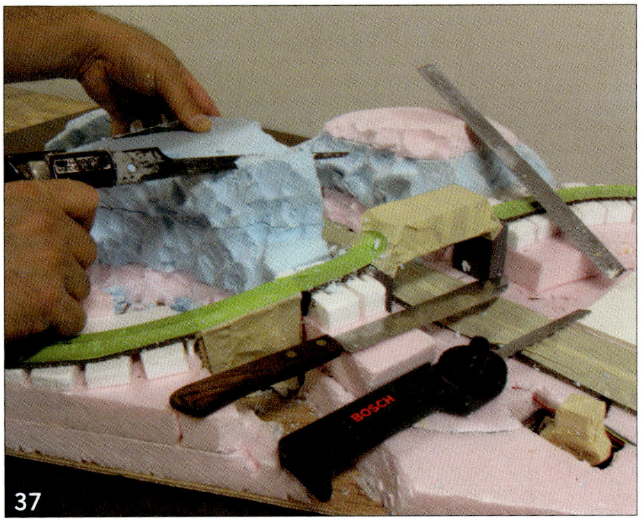

37

The foam can be shaped with a keyhole saw, serrated knives (foreground), and a rasp (leaning on the mountain).

38

Blend rocks and foam joints with lightweight spackling. Water, a screwdriver, and a sponge are handy for working the spackling.

39

Start coloring rocks with a base coat of beige (right). Dab on craft paints (middle), then blend the colors with a brush (left). The cup of water is handy to help blend colors and clean brushes.

40

To make realistic water, use a brush to work gloss medium along the surface and into the details of the creek bed.

instructions to install the wiring corresponding to the method your club uses—either the traditional scheme with cinch-jones connectors or the newer system with heavier wire and "power pole" connectors. My club uses the latter, **30**.

See the schematic for private track wiring, **31**. Refer back to **4** for the location of track feeder wires. All wiring will run through a connector to allow disassembly. I concealed this connector with a building that can be removed to facilitate mating the connectors. You could use a removable scenic feature instead of a structure to hide the connector. If you are not making the coffee table to house this layout in Chapter 4, the connector can simply hang below the layout at any location except where the lift-out sits on the cross members.

I used a nine-pin connector since it was the smallest I could find with the necessary seven connection points. Extend 22-gauge wire from the track and the switch machines to one end of the connector. Solder or crimp all wire connections, depending on which type of connector you use. Extend wires from the other end of the connector to the Atlas Twin controller, the switch machine controller, and, in turn, to the power pack. Leave enough slack in the wires for the control box to be mounted on either side of the frame or clamped to the rolling base leg.

Note that I only use one switch machine controller to operate both turnouts at once, but two could be used to allow independent turnout control. If using one, wire both turnouts to throw to the same side of the passing siding. As explained earlier, the Atlas Twin allows you to turn off power to one side of the passing siding to stage one train while you run on the other side, **32**.

Painting the rail and ties gives them a realistic appearance and helps hide the rail's out-of-scale size. First, paint all of the ties and rail sides a dark brown color, but avoid the moving parts of the turnouts. Wipe the rail tops as you go. When dry, paint the rail sides a rusty color, **33**. I used inexpensive craft paints, which are available for various different manufacturers from arts and crafts stores. Water-based model railroad paints also work well.

You can also weather track with spray paint from a low angle (after covering turnouts and donning a respirator), but I felt it was not worth the expense or mess on this small of a layout. One other option is Floquil's three-pack of organic solvent-based track weathering markers. You may also simulate oil and grease drippings along the centers of the tie tops with gray and black paint. Finally, remove any remaining paint from rail heads with an abrasive track cleaner.

Scenery and rockwork

To add scenery to the lift-out section, it is best to remove it from the module frame. The first step is to tape over all the track to protect it before the messy fun begins, **34**.

Cut down into the 1" foam base with a knife for the river—right down to the plywood. Then use pieces of rigid extruded foam to build your mountain forms. This type of foam can be chipped away to make rock faces. Alternatively, you could refer to scenery books for other methods such as plaster castings, but they are heavier and subject to breakage on a portable layout.

When you are satisfied with the general shape of the stacked pieces of foam, glue them to each other and to the layout with construction adhesive. Weight the stacks down temporarily while the glue dries.

Bill of materials

Lumber
- 1 x 2, 8' pine
- 1 x 4, 6' pine, 3 (two if using the drawer from Chapter 4 for controls)
- 2 x 4, 6' pine, 2 **
- 2 x 2, 8' pine, 2
- ¼" plywood, 4' x 4' sheet

Hardware
- * 1¼" drywall screws
- 2½" deck screws, 8 **
- No. 8 x ¾" sheet metal screws, 20 **
- No. 6 x ½" sheet-metal screws, 8
- ¼" tee nuts, 4
- ¼" x 3" carriage bolts, 4
- Casters with appropriate hardware, 4 **
- ¼" x 3" flathead bolts, flat washers and matching wing nuts, 4
- No. 10 x 1½" roundhead bolts, flat washers, and matching wing nuts, 3
- ¼" x 2" flathead bolts, flat washers, and matching wing nuts, 2

Track
- Atlas no. 2702 (remote right turnout), 2
- Atlas no. 2546 truss bridge
- Atlas no. 2532 rerailers, 2
- Atlas no. 2500 flextrack, 8
- Atlas no. 2535 rail joiners
- Chooch Enterprises no. 9760 random stone, single-track tunnel portals (for stone arch bridge), 2

Electrical
- Atlas no. 311 power pack
- Atlas no. 210 Twin
- Radio Shack no. 274-229 nine-pin connector (male)
- Radio Shack no. 274-239 nine-pin connector (female)
- * 22-gauge stranded wire
- * wiring and connectors as necessary for the Ntrak wiring mode of choice (see text)

Scenery
- Instant Horizons backdrop no. 706
- Instant Horizons backdrop no. 707
- Woodland Scenics no. B73 ballast (fine buff)
- 1" extruded foam, 24" x 48" sheet
- * additional extruded foam for track inclines and mountain stacks
- * Brawa plastic sheet material (stone or block) for retaining walls
- ¼" styrene tube (for drain pipe)
- * Lightweight spackling
- * Matte medium
- * Gloss medium
- * Ground foam, various
- * Sculptamold
- $\frac{3}{16}$" foam core

Structures
- Pola no. N240 Werkhalle (workshop)
- Pola no. N211 Loco Shed
- Model Power no. 1525 Baldwin Loco Works
- Model Power no. 1510 Star Journal
- Walthers Cornerstone no. 3224 Merchants Row II

Miscellaneous
- Cork roadbed, 28'
- Latex wood primer
- Flat latex beige paint,
- Semi-gloss latex black or brown paint
- * Wood glue
- * Masking tape

* Quantity as needed or desired
** Only needed for rolling base

As in earlier chapters, make the roads and the structure bases from $\frac{3}{16}$"-thick foam core. After cutting it to shape, remove a bit of the foam and bottom facing near the track/roadbed edge for a smooth transition at the crossings. Glue the foam core in place with construction adhesive and weight it down to dry. In between the rails at the crossings, glue a piece of the foam core facing (below rail height). The foam core, foam stacks for the mountains, and cutout for the river can all be seen in **35**.

When you're sure the adhesive is dry (probably a few days), shape the rock faces by chipping away with a chisel, scraper, or even a flat screwdriver, **36**. After pulling away chunks of foam, you are left with a realistic rock surface. Shape the tops of the foam stacks with

The kids fishing seem to be oblivious to the trains coming through.

a knife, a rasp, or any other tool you prefer to get the effect you desire, **37**. Looking from different angles can help while you are shaping the contours.

At the face of the incline on the left where the private track is elevated just to the rear of the Ntrak main lines, I added a block retaining wall using Brawa plastic sheet material, **3**. I painted and weathered the sheet before cutting it to fit. You could instead carve a rock face here, but again, I wanted variety for visual interest. I also used some stone sheet material at both ends of the creek.

Apply lightweight spackling to blend in all areas. This material is lightweight and simple to use—it's like frosting a cake, **38**. Fill between the spaces on the track inclines, foam joints, and around road and structure bases. Leave the rock faces as the bare chipped foam as much as possible, since it yields a nice rough look when painted. However, be sure to disguise the horizontal joints between levels of foam. Sculptamold could be used either as an alternative to the spackling or where a rougher texture is desired.

After all the scenery base is dry, give it a coat of beige latex paint. When dry, paint the rock faces with the colors you desire, depending on the area you are modeling. I like to use craft paints for this as well, **39**. You can either make diluted washes by mixing the paint with water or brush different colors on here and there, then wash them down with water in a spray bottle or with a wet brush. I prefer to combine different methods to vary the scenery and achieve different effects. Experiment with this—it's impossible to make mistakes, simply because you can paint over anything you don't like with the base coat and start over.

Final scenery

See the previous chapters for techniques on road painting and the construction of sidewalks and structures. I used a colored pencil for the road center lines. If you prefer not to build structures from kits, Atlas markets a

This view from inside the layout at an Ntrak setup shows club member Jim Altobello's train coming through the PU module.

T-trak is an outgrowth of Ntrak. One-foot-square modules are set on table tops. How can you say you don't have room for one of these?

line of assembled and painted structures. Remember, for access I did not glue down the building that conceals the connector.

Apply ground cover as shown in Chapter 1, but with one difference: Use matte medium spray instead of paint to apply the first layer of ground foam on the mountain tops. This prevents you from messing up your rock faces. Remember to scenic the fixed section forward of the Ntrak lines. You can then ballast all the track as shown in Chapter 2.

The final scenic element is the creek. Use the same colors you used for the rock faces to paint the creek bed, with darker colors in the middle, fading to lighter hues at the creek edges. At the ends of the creek, where you already installed stone retaining walls, add a pre-painted section of ¼" styrene tubing to simulate a drain pipe. Place assorted rocks and twigs into the creek bed. When satisfied, glue them with matte medium solution. When it's dry, add gloss medium for the water. This goes on white like matte medium, but dries to a clear gloss, **40**. You can add multiple coats of gloss medium to build up the stream, allowing drying time between. Thin coats will help prevent bubbles from remaining in your creek. Before the last coat of gloss medium, dry-brush white paint downstream of rocks to simulate white water, **41**.

Add trees, figures, vehicles, and other details. I used some highly detailed foreground trees from Woodland Scenics. Finally, prime and paint the outside of the layout frame and all legs with black or brown paint per Ntrak standards.

Rolling stock and setup

Only two Ntrak legs are needed to stabilize the layout if you leave it on the rolling base frame at home. In this case, you will need to cut a notch out of the backdrop (**6**) to fit around the rolling base upright member. You will also want to clamp the control box to the layout frame or rolling base for best access to controls.

Standard rolling stock will work fine on the tight curves, especially with truck-mounted couplers that are standard on much N scale rolling stock. Due to the tighter-than-standard curves, smaller engines and rolling stock (50 feet or shorter) will look and perform best.

To add personality to this layout, you can decal your fleet for the Pacific Union by reversing Union Pacific decals, **42**.

Possible variations

- Add 6" to the rear of the module, as is optional in Ntrak specifications. This will allow you to use broader radius curves.
- Add spur tracks in various locations for switching.
- Make as many interchangeable lift-out sections as you'd like.
- To leave the backdrop on while the layout is folded on the rolling base, increase the length of member M to 27⅜".
- Make a T-trak module, **43**.
- Use leg pockets and metal legs as shown in Chapter 7 or folding legs as in Chapter 9.

1

CHAPTER FOUR

The Pacific Union Extension

A coffee table holding the lift-out layout section from Chapter 3

A coffee table provides an excellent space for showing off a small layout.

As I explained in Chapter 3, the Ntrak module is already two layouts in one, serving for both modular group setups and as a home layout. My goal was to develop a more presentable way to display and use that removable layout. The result is a coffee table with a glass top to house it, **1**. The slide-in design and removable wire connector make the transition very simple, **2**. You could, of course, make the removable section in Chapter 3 for use only in this coffee table, and disregard the remainder of the Ntrak module in that chapter, **3**.

I used poplar wood to achieve a nice finish, after finding that is was only a bit more expensive than clear pine, and readily available in home centers such as Lowe's. You could substitute any other wood of the same dimensions.

Basic box and leg assembly

Cut all of the box members (A, B, C, D, and E) to size. The plans and cutting diagram are illustrated in **4** and **5**. I cut member A (the box bottom) from an 18" x 48" edge-glued board. If you cannot find such a board, you may also cut member A from a 2' x 4' sheet of plywood. Mark and cut the wire access hole in member A, using the actual layout as a guide. If you would like to be able to slide the layout in facing in either direction, make two holes—I didn't think of this until later in the construction process. Both holes are shown in **4** and **11**.

2

The layout slides into the table from the side. This layout is the removable Pacific Union section from the Ntrak module shown in Chapter 3.

3

Here's a low-level view of the downtown area. The convertible and the tire change scene are from Woodland Scenics, which offers many detail items as well as scenery materials.

Table and drawer plans

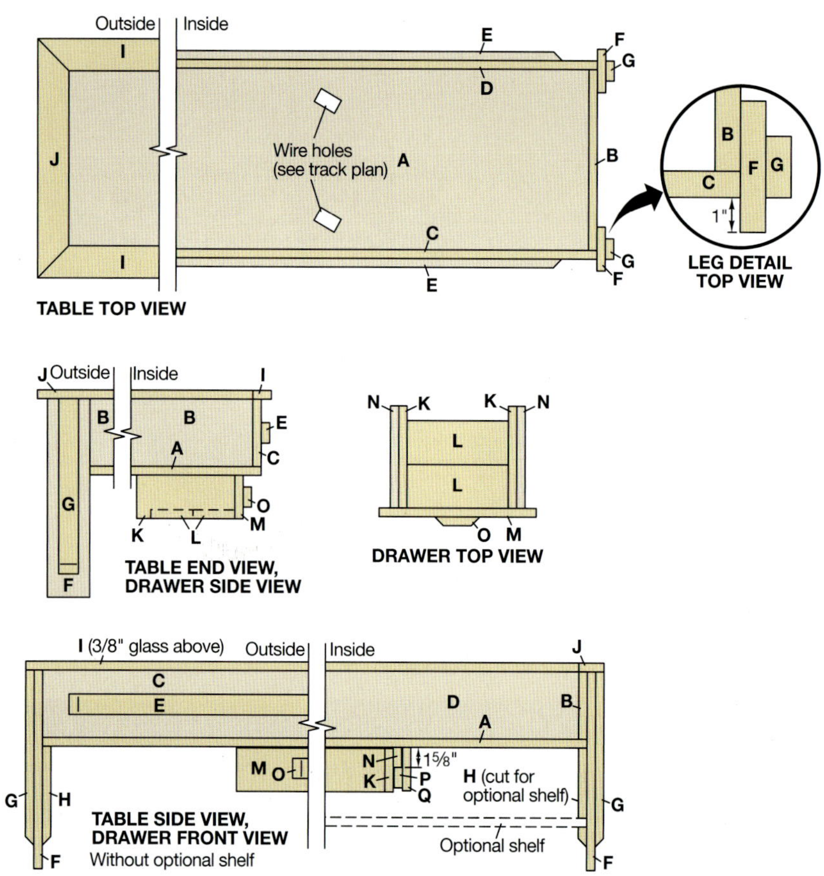

4

Cutting Diagram

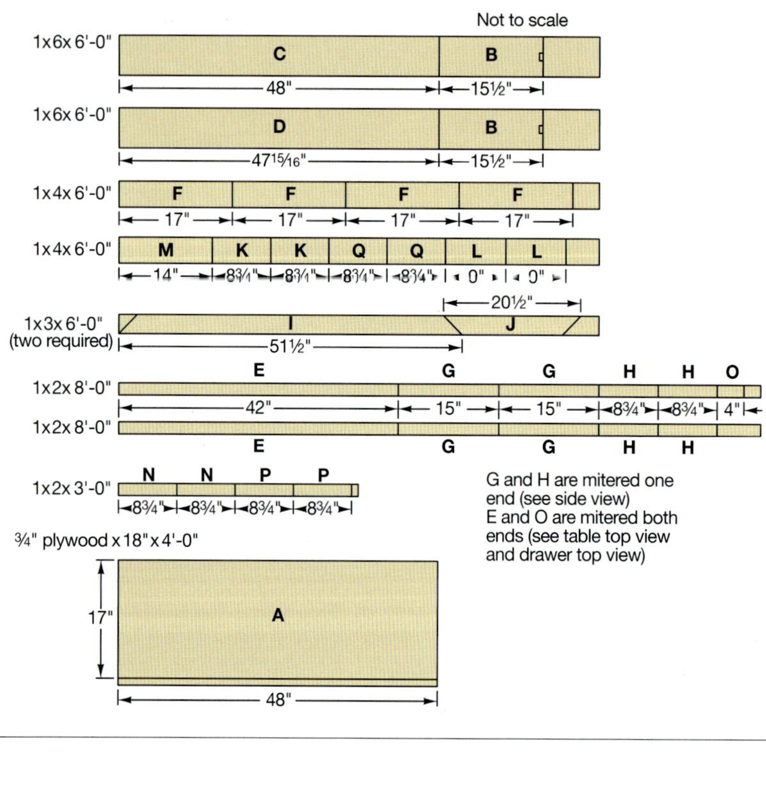

5

Cut notches out of ends B. These notches will eventually house the magnetic catches that will hold the removable side later. Size the notches to fit the catches you purchase, **6**.

Begin assembly by fastening ends B to bottom A with 1¼" drywall screws and wood glue. Countersink these and all other screw and nail holes in this project to allow them to be concealed later. Then fasten long side C to members A and B with the same screws and wood glue, **6**. This will be the fixed side. Fasten one trim member E to side C with 1¼" finishing nails and wood glue. I chose nails for this because the strength of screws is not needed, and nail holes are smaller to conceal. For the removable side, fasten the other trim member E to side D with nails and glue, but do not fasten this to the box assembly, **7**.

Before cutting the leg parts, decide if you are adding the optional shelf, **4**. Cut leg parts F, G, and H to length. If you are adding the shelf, cut members H into two pieces—each the proper length to allow for the thickness of the shelf and to account for the level at which you would like it.

Fasten all four legs F to the box assembly with 1¼" drywall screws and wood glue. Make sure the legs extend horizontally 1" past the box assembly as shown in **4**. If you are adding the shelf, fasten it to the box now with 1¼" drywall screws and wood glue. Nail and glue the trim pieces G to the outside of all legs with 1¼" finishing nails, **8**. Do the same with trim pieces H to the insides of the legs. Countersink all nails, **9**. Be sure to provide good support behind each member while nailing and countersinking.

Now go back and retrieve the removable side assembly (member D with trim piece E). This is shorter than the fixed one by ¹⁄₁₆" in length to allow easy removal. You will also need to plane one long edge of member D to narrow it down enough to slide in and out easily. If you have access to an edger, take advantage of it; otherwide a plane will do the job well. Sanding will also work, but will be quite time consuming. This is the most demanding part of construction, so grin, turn

This is the basic box assembly, with the removable side on the left. The arrow on the right points to the notch where the catch will be recessed. The arrow on the left shows the location of the hole for the wire connector.

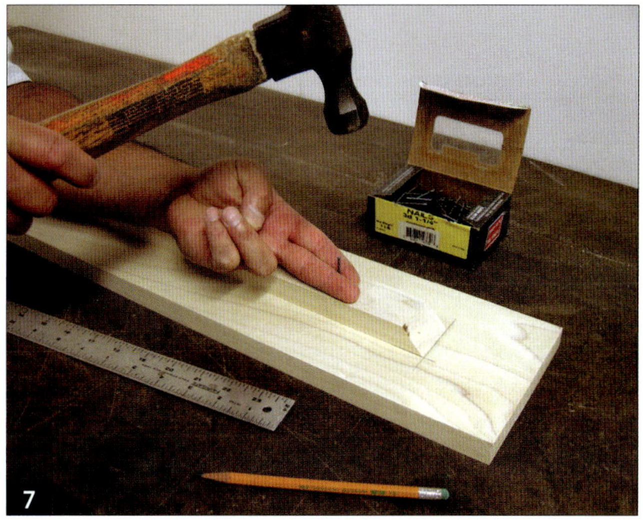

Install trim on the removable side. This is the correct way to hold a nail while hammering it in—a missed swing will sting a little, but won't crush your fingernail. You could also hold the nail in position with needlenose pliers to start it.

Nail the trim to one of the legs (right). Before I fastened the legs to the box (with screws), I marked the future location of the trim piece so the screws would be hidden by the trim. On the left, you can see this, as well as where I cross-hatched off the area overhanging the box and the area notched out for the catch to indicate where I should not drive the screws.

After nailing one of the leg trim pieces in place (while the table is on its end), countersink the nails (drive the heads below the top surface) with a nail set. On the right is the wood putty which will eventually conceal all nail and screw holes.

on some good music, and bear it. Trim piece E serves as a handle for the removable side.

Install the magnetic portion of the catches to the legs (members F) within the notches in box ends (members B). Install the metal plates that mate with the catch on the inside of the removable side assembly, **10**.

Cut top members I and J to length. Make the miter joints as neat as possible, since they will show through the glass top. Fasten all four top members to the box assembly with 1¼" drywall screws and wood glue, ending with the top piece above the removable side. Under this last top piece, you will see that there is not much leg surface to accept the screws, so drill and install carefully, and at a slight angle, to keep the wood from splitting, **11**. Then, to strengthen all four corners of the mitered top, drive 1¼" nails horizontally through each joint, from both directions, **12**. Drill ¹⁄₁₆" pilot holes for these nails to prevent the wood from splitting. Offset the nails in each corner a bit so they are at slightly different levels—if the second one strikes the first, they may drive the joint out of alignment vertically. Also, if the joint is out of alignment vertically before nailing, clamp the joint into alignment, using scrap blocks above and below, before driving the nails.

Drawer

A drawer may seem like an intimidating thing to build if you have never

This close-up shows the magnetic catch fastened to the leg within the notch cut from the box end. On the right is the removable side with the metal plate fastened in position to mate with the catch.

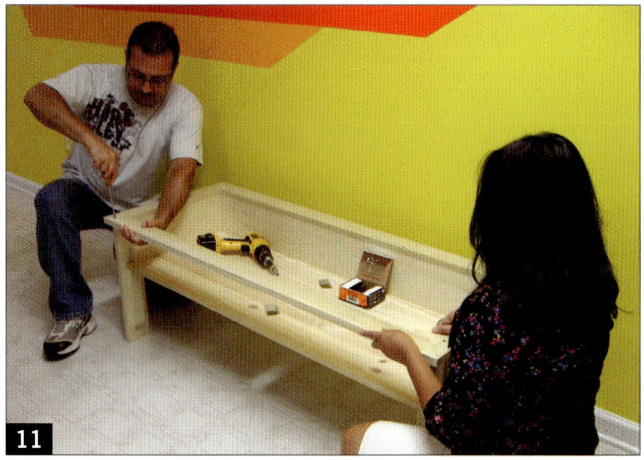

With my wife, Erna, helping, I am carefully installing the last of the mitered top pieces—the one spanning the removable side. You can see by the angle of my screwdriver that I have angled the screws slightly to reach farther from the edge of the leg. You can also see both wire holes in box bottom A, which allows the layout to slide into place facing either direction.

To strengthen the miter joints, especially above the removable side, drive a nail in each direction sideways to lock the joint in place. To keep the wood from splitting, I used the drill shown to pre-drill 1⁄16" holes about ½" deep to accept the nails.

Here's the drawer and the runners, prior to installation of the drawer front in the foreground.

I am fastening one of the runners to the box bottom. My wife again proves to be indispensable—this time to hold the runner in place.

Apply putty to all of the screw holes.

16

Once the putty dries, sand the areas so they are smooth and flush with the wood surface.

17

Prime the table, then paint it the final color. Two coats may be necessary to completely cover the primer.

18

Add mounting pads for the glass top.

19

Replace the removable side after sliding the layout into the table.

made one before, but fear not! I have designed a drawer that uses stock lumber widths and all butt joints, **13**. Cut members K, L, M, N, and O to size first for the drawer itself. Fasten sides K to bottom pieces L with 1¼" finishing nails and wood glue. Place front member M centered on the assembly and use 1¼" drywall screws and wood glue to fasten it to members K and L. Nail and glue members N to the outsides of the drawer as shown to ride on the runners. Fasten handle O from the inside of the drawer with 1¼" drywall screws and wood glue.

Now build the runners after cutting members P and Q to length. Nail and glue members P to members Q with member P 1⅝" from the top of member Q. The runners are also shown in **13**. Fasten these runner assemblies to the underside of the box bottom (member A) with 1¼" drywall screws and glue, **14**. Make sure the runners are located 12⅛" apart such that the drawer is centered on the table. I inset them approximately 1½" from the edge of member A to allow the drawer front to be set back ¾" from the box side when closed. I installed the runner assemblies on the side of the table opposite the removable side to allow control from the couch side and layout removal from the opposite side. You may choose either side.

Mount the controls in the drawer just as shown back in Chapter 3 (**3-32**). If you are using this layout with the Ntrak module in Chapter 3, you can use this drawer with the controls for Ntrak setups instead of the control box in Chapter 3. The drawer is sized to mount in the Ntrak frame—simply substitute ¼" x 3" bolts for mounting.

Finishing

Make sure all screws and nails are countersunk, then fill all holes with sandable wood putty, **15**. Avoid the temptation to fill the miter joints with putty—my experience tells me that the putty will eventually crack due to wood expansion and contraction. When the putty is dry, sand the areas flush to their respective surfaces, with progressively finer sandpaper, down to at least 220 grit, **16**. Remove all sanding residue—preferably with a tack cloth.

Give all surfaces a coat of wood primer. When that dries, sand any

20

The entire family gathers around the coffee-table layout. The table blends in nicely with the other furniture in the room.

Bill of materials

Lumber
- Edge-glued board (two if optional shelf is desired), 18" x 48"
- 1 x 6, 6' poplar, 2
- 1 x 4, 6' poplar, 2
- 1 x 3, 6' poplar, 2
- 1 x 2, 8' poplar, 2
- 1 x 2, 3' poplar

Hardware
* 1¼" finishing nails
* 1¼" drywall screws (preferably coarse)
- Magnetic catches, 2
- ¼" x 3" flathead bolts, washers, and wing nuts (if using drawer with Ntrak layout in Chapter 3), 2

Miscellaneous
- Water-based wood primer
- Water-based semi-gloss black paint
* Wood glue
* Sandpaper
- Glass top, 21" x 52"
- Glass-mounting pads, 6

* quantity as needed or desired

rough spots lightly with 220 grit or finer sandpaper. Try not to reveal any bare wood. Once you remove the sanding residue, apply the final paint color, **17**. Two or three coats may be necessary for coverage. Multiple thin coats are better than a single thick one to prevent the paint from running or dripping. You may of course choose to a color other than black, or you can apply stain and varnish as shown in Chapter 5.

After everything is thoroughly dry and you are satisfied with the finish, place mounting pads for the glass on the top of the wood table surfaces in the corners above the legs, **18**, and the middle of each long side. The glass I used is ⅜" thick with plain, polished edges. A local glass supplier (check online or in the Yellow Pages) will be able to cut a piece of glass to any size you need. You can have your glass supplier provide fancier edges—for the right price, of course. Place the glass on the table and stand back to admire your work.

Now the table is ready for use. Slide the layout in, snap the wire connector in place from below, and then replace the removable side, **19**. Use caution with the power cord. Since it must be run to a wall outlet, locate it to minimize tripping, but do not run it under anything which could create a fire hazard. It's usually best to leave it unplugged except when running the layout, **20, 21**.

Variations

• Instead of building a table, you can purchase a table to house a layout, **22**.

• Use this coffee table concept for any layout by adjusting the box dimension to fit the layout you'd like. Many N scale track plans have been published for a 2' x 4' space. HO switching

21

The kids fishing can feel the rumble of the trains. Looks like the local fire inspector has arrived to check out the business on the right.

layouts such as the one in Chapter 2 are similar in size.

• Build a non-removable layout into the coffee table. If you do, change dimensions of the removable side D to be the same as side C. Remember, you'll then need to lift off the top to access the trains, and I'd then recommend a lighter acrylic top such as the one shown in Chapter 5 instead of heavy glass.

• Employ the same concept for a dining table by enlarging both the box dimensions and the leg lengths.

• Add a second drawer for storage.

• Use a table to display trains only, without a drawer.

• Adjust the height of the table by changing the height of the legs and associated trim pieces. Standard height is 16" to 18". A common rule-of-thumb is the same height (or 1" to 2" lower) than the adjacent seating.

22

Many commercially available tables have a shadow-box area that could house a layout.

1

CHAPTER FIVE

The Brookeville Division

An N scale layout built into an end table

This complete, detailed layout suitable for display or operation fits nicely into an end table measuring only 2 x 3 feet.

Here is another easily-built piece of furniture to house a layout. In this case, the layout is permanently built in. Remember the philosophy I mentioned in the introduction regarding layouts in furniture—that they take no room because they can still serve their function as the piece of furniture, **1**. The cover I use in this chapter is a piece of acrylic plastic that can be removed for access, **2**.

The theme of the layout is a short line serving a typical small town. It connects to a larger rail system by means of the interchange track in the corner. This is one of the smallest N scale layouts possible using Atlas sectional track that can include a passing siding and interior spurs, **3**. It is a modified version of layout N-2 in the Atlas book *Introduction to N Scale Model Railroading*.

As in Chapter 3, the passing siding is electrically blocked to allow two trains to be on the layout, and either one can be run at any given time. I use remote control turnouts and remote block controls to allow full operation while the layout is covered.

Main layout frame and legs

The wood I chose for the visible pieces of this project is clear poplar, for the same reasons as in Chapter 4. You could use nicer wood such as oak, which is also available in home centers such as Lowe's. Choose whatever wood and finish you prefer, perhaps to match other furniture pieces. The plans are shown in **4**, **5**, and **6**.

I used 45-degree miter joints in the corners of the frame for appearance. It is difficult to obtain good-fitting miter joints like this with a hand miter box or portable power tools. If you do not have the experience or tools (a table saw or power miter saw) to cut miter joints, either have them cut for you, or substitute butt joints. To do this, simply change the length of member A to 36", cut members A and B square, and assemble, **4**.

Whichever type of joint you choose, assemble the four outside frame members (A and B) with 1¼" finishing nails and wood glue, **7**. Countersink nail heads and putty the holes.

Cut the plywood bottom (member C) to size and drill the wiring holes as indicated in **6**. Place the bottom into the frame on a flat surface. Now cut the ¾" square blocking and fasten it to the outside frame members with no. 8 x 1¼" flathead wood screws and wood glue, **8**.

Turn the assembly over and attach the plywood to the blocking with no. 8 x 1" flathead wood screws, **9**). Don't use glue for this, in case you need to access wiring later.

2

The Brookeville Depot receives a flatcar load of new tractors.

The legs I use are available in different lengths and come with mounting plates. Start by mounting the plates onto the plywood bottom with appropriate hardware, **9**. I used no. 10 x ½" sheet-metal screws because they have round heads, course threads, and are available in short lengths. After this, simply screw the legs onto the mounting plates.

Drawer and frame

Again, I have designed a drawer that uses stock lumber and all butt joints. It does not follow typical furniture drawer construction, but it is strong enough to hold the control items we need.

The first step is the construction of the three-sided frame into which the drawer slides. Cut members D and E; remember the notch in member E for the power supply wire. Glue and nail members D to member E with 1¼" finishing nails. Then fasten the plywood bottom of the frame (member F) using glue and the same nails, **10**. Countersink and putty all nails.

Finally, attach this entire assembly to the main layout box where shown in **4**. Use wood glue and no. 8 x 1¼" flathead wood screws through box bottom C, **11**).

Now proceed to the drawer itself. Remember to cut the notches out of members H and I. The notch in member H faces the top of the drawer and allows the drawer to be opened past the wiring. The notch in member I faces the bottom of the drawer and is needed for clearance around the handle mounting screws. Check your handle for exact dimensions of this notch.

Track and wiring diagram

KEY

- ↑ = Power feed (one rail)—from Atlas selector
- ↕ = Power feed (both rails)—directly from power pack
- ■ = Insulated joiner (one rail)
- ⊖ = Uncoupling magnet
- R = Right turnout
- L = Left turnout
- B = Bumper
- 5 = 5" Straight
- 2½" = 2½" Straight (from assortment)
- 1¼" = 1¼" Straight (from assortment)
- ¼ = ¼" Straight (from assortment)
- 19 = 19" Radius (from turnout packages)
- BR = Bridge
- RR = Rerailer

Unmarked sections are 9¾" radius

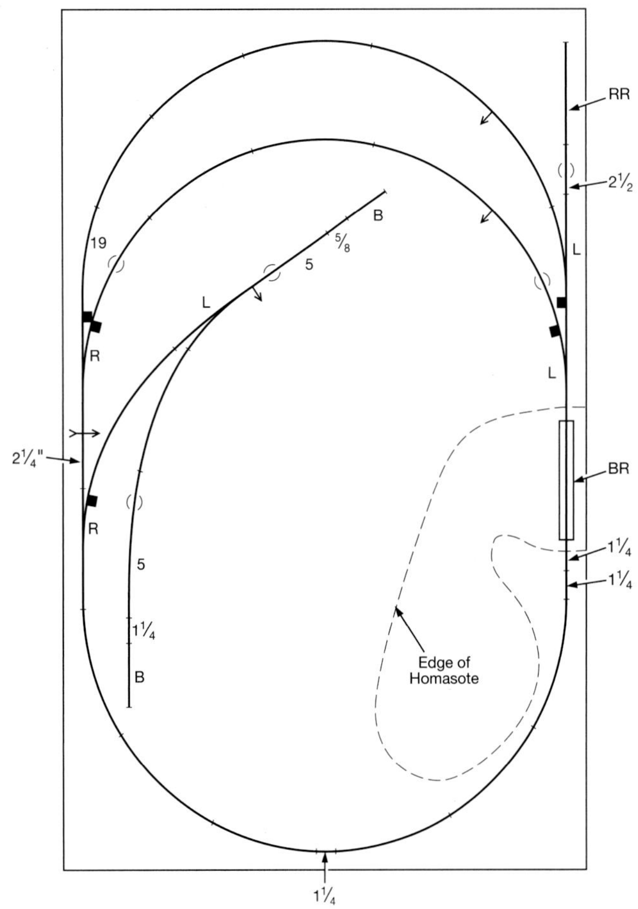

3

Make a four-sided box from members G, H, and I using glue and 4d finishing nails. Attach the drawer bottom, member J, with glue and 1" wire brads. Countersink all nails and brads; putty is optional, **12**. Study the drawings (**4**, **5**) carefully to make sure all members are oriented correctly.

Drill the holes for the handle hardware so the handle is centered on the drawer face, member K. Fasten the face to the drawer assembly with four no. 8 x 1¼" flathead wood screws from the inside, **13**, and attach the handler.

If you are really paying attention, you may have noticed an apparent problem. The vertical drawer dimensions total up to the exact 3½"opening in the drawer frame. Don't worry: ½"plywood is actually 15/32" thick, giving us 1/16" of slack to enable movement of the drawer.

Now sand all of the wood surfaces. Start with medium (100) grit or coarser paper if necessary. Repeat the process thoroughly with progressively finer sandpaper, to at least 220 grit, until you are satisfied with the smoothness of the surfaces. Wipe off all sanding dust with a tack cloth.

Stain and finish the outside surfaces using the products of your choice according to their instructions, **14**. I find it easiest to use the newer generation of stains and finishes that can be wiped or sprayed on. They are easier to control and there will be no brushes to clean. The poly/oil finish I used is from the Woodworker's Store; similar products are available from Constantine's (see the suppliers and manufacturers section in the appendix). Water-based products are also available if you prefer.

Apply a wood primer to the inside surfaces of the box sides. When dry, paint these areas with the same flat beige paint used for the scenery base coat. Keep all primer and paint off the stained surfaces. After the scenery is complete, touch up the paint inside the box sides.

Roadbed, track, and wiring

Cut a piece of Homasote measuring 22⅞" x 35⅞" and make the irregular cut for the river and lake, **3**. Install additional ¾" square blocking on the box bottom to support the middle of the Homasote. You can see this blocking ahead in **19**. Wait to fasten the Homasote until after you install, test, and paint the track. Adjustments will be much easier.

Assemble the sectional track on the Homasote and mark the track center lines, **15**. Remove the track and install the cork roadbed as shown in Chapter 3. If you want to paint the bridge (as I did—with a silver color), do that now before reinstallation. Then spike all track down as shown in Chapter 1, remembering to install the insulated joiners as shown in the track plan. The 19" radius section was not included on the bill of materials because it came with the turnouts.

Solder all track connections and power feeder wires to the outsides of the appropriate rail sections as described in Chapter 3. Connection points for the track power wires are shown on the track plan. Connect all track wires temporarily to the power pack and test all track thoroughly. Then paint the track as in Chapter 3.

Main layout box

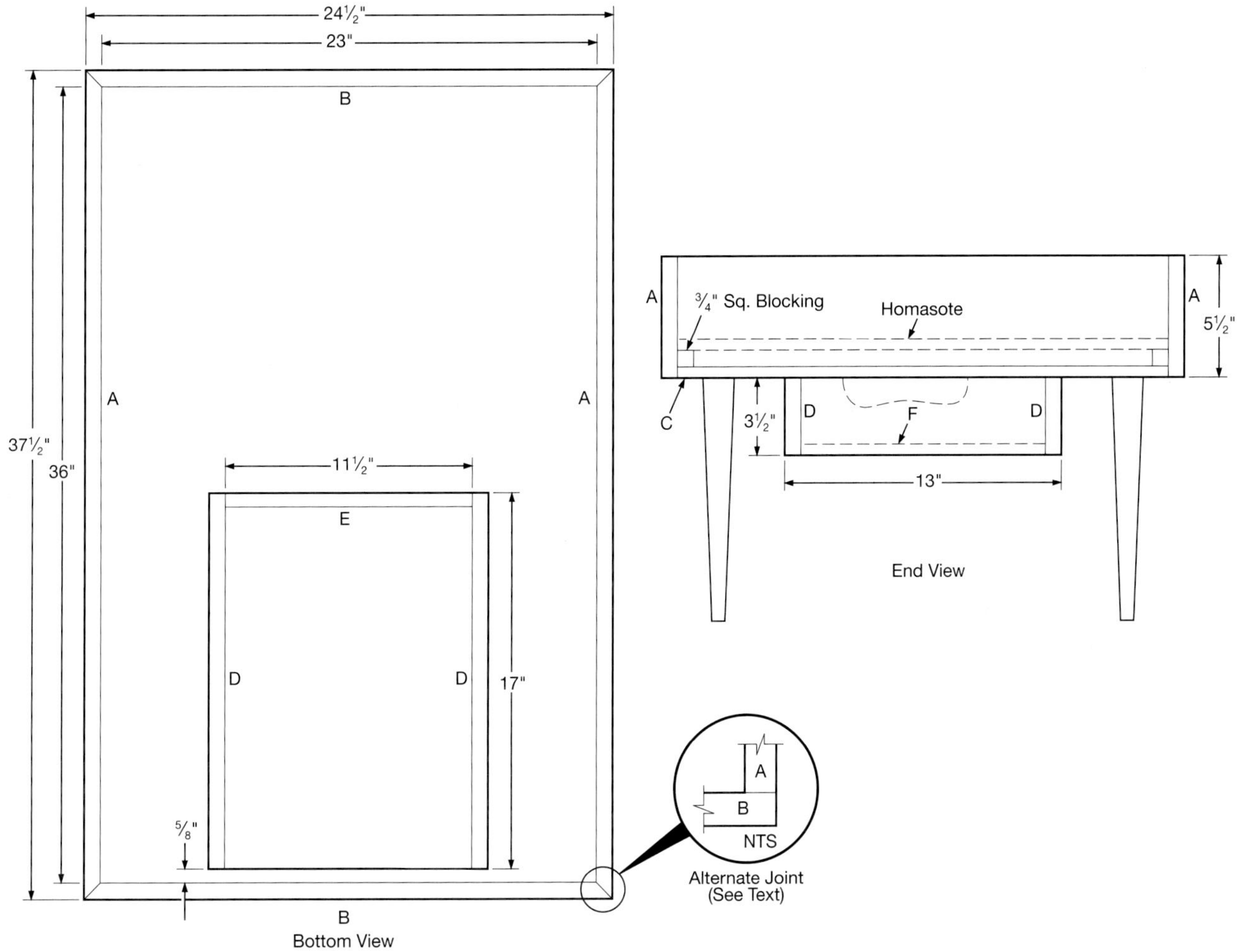

4

Now is the time to install the magnets which will be used for remote uncoupling later, **3**. Follow the detailed instructions included with the Micro-Trains permanent magnets. I cut them in half as per the instructions to better fit in curved track. This also minimizes accidental uncoupling with shorter rolling stock.

Extend each set of turnout control wires with 24-gauge, three-conductor wire to reach the outer end of the drawer when it is extended. I used Radio Shack's no. 278-871 wire, which comes with an outer jacket. Solder and tape all connections. Do this carefully to minimize the chance you'll need to get to these connections in the future.

Now fasten all of the wiring to the Homasote with insulated cable staples, **16**. Carefully ease the wire through

Drawer plans

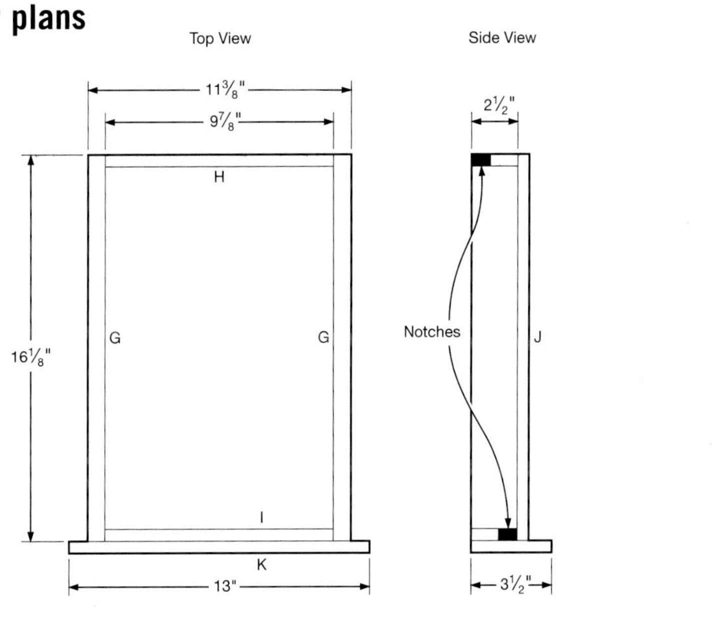

5

Cutting diagrams

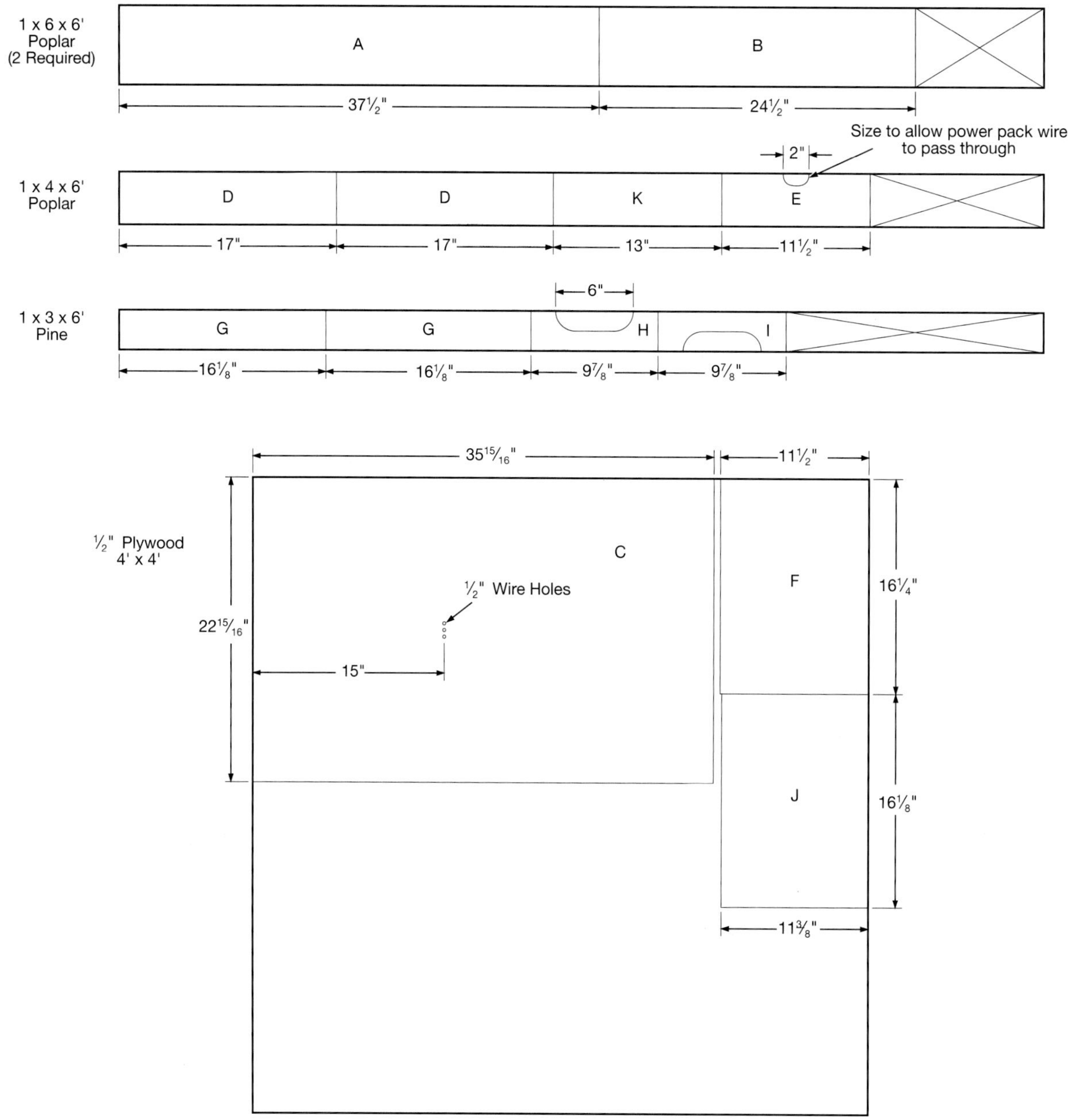

6

the box bottom while lowering the Homasote into place.

Place the power pack into the drawer and pass the 120V cord through the hole in the drawer frame. Mount the Atlas Selector and the turnout controls in the drawer, **17**, attaching them with the screws included. I arranged the turnout controls in the same pattern as the corresponding turnouts while you are facing the layout. Connect all wires per the Atlas instructions and the track plan and bundle the wires, **17**.

Now fasten the track/Homasote assembly into the layout box with no. 8 x 1" flathead wood screws. Keep a record of where these screws are located in case you need to access wiring after the scenery conceals the screws. For the bridge abutments, cut 1¼" square blocks from a scrap piece of 1 x 3, prime and paint them, and glue them under each end of the bridge, **19**.

Scenery and structures

The scenery is mostly done with the same techniques and methods demonstrated in Chapters 1, 2, and 3, with some new materials. One variation is to use pieces of suspended ceiling tile instead of foam to build mountain areas, **20**. Use cellulose-based rigid tiles, not the spongy fiber glass-based tiles. When the cellulose type tiles are broken instead of cut through, the edges simulate interesting rock faces, **21**.

Assemble the box sides with nails and glue. Note the carpenter's square being used to maintain 90-degree corners. If you do not have a band clamp, you'll need an extra set of hands for this.

The plywood bottom simply sits inside the box sides while you fasten the blocking to the sides. You can see the river area marked and blocking omitted at that point along the side.

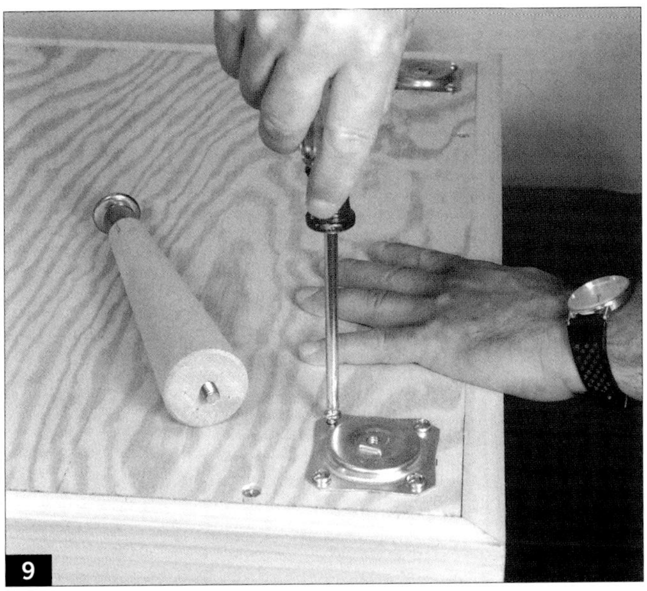

Here is the box bottom after the plywood has been fastened to the blocking from below. Attach the mounting plates for the legs into the plywood with their centers 2½" in from the sides. In the end of the leg, you can see the threaded stud that turns into the mounting plate.

Use glue and nails to assemble the frame that holds the drawer. Be careful to drive the nails straight in to avoid splitting the plywood.

Make the banks for the lake and river out of Sculptamold, **22**. Install two pieces of pre-painted drinking straw or styrene tubing to serve as drain pipes. Finish the banks and the other rock faces as in Chapter 3.

Make roads with Durham's Water Putty. Follow the directions on the container. This material goes on very nicely with a putty knife (wet if necessary). This product dries to a color that resembles fresh concrete. Carve some cracks in the road with your hobby knife if you wish. Paint the surfaces a concrete or asphalt color or leave them unpainted as I did here. Weather the roads with powdered chalk if you'd like.

After building the structures, install them, **23**, with matte medium. When applying ground cover, be sure to wipe off any matte medium solution that may have been sprayed on the finished portions of the layout frame. Weather the road with powdered chalk.

When the rest of the scenery is done, paint the lake bed flat black, feathering it with beige around the edges, **24**. Glue debris such as weeds and rocks around the lake edges as you desire. Follow the Woodland Scenics E-Z Water instructions for adding water to the lake bed, **25**. Be careful not to melt the bridge if you use a heat gun to soften the E-Z Water. You could also substitute gloss medium for the water as in Chapter 3.

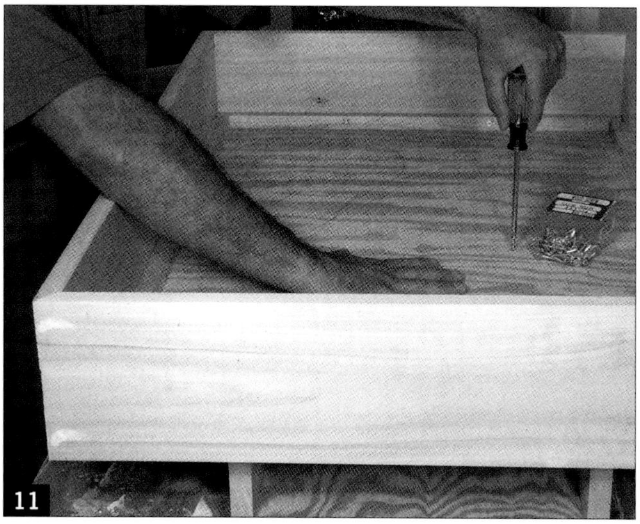

11 Fasten the drawer frame (below) to the layout box.

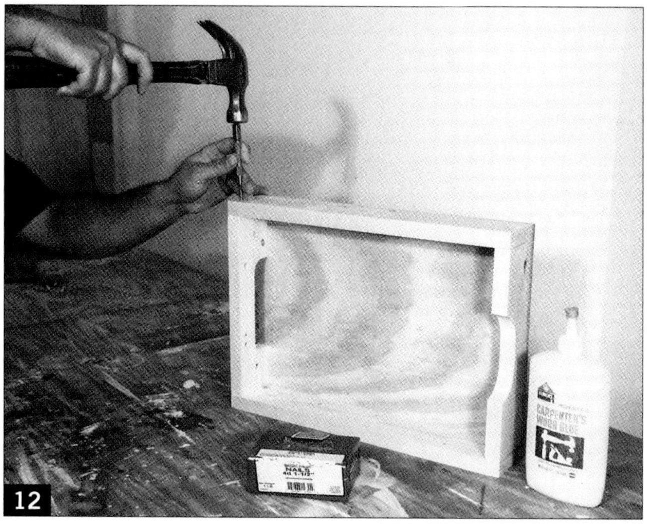

12 Assemble the drawer with nails and glue, making sure that the notches face the correct direction. Use a nail set as shown to countersink the nail heads.

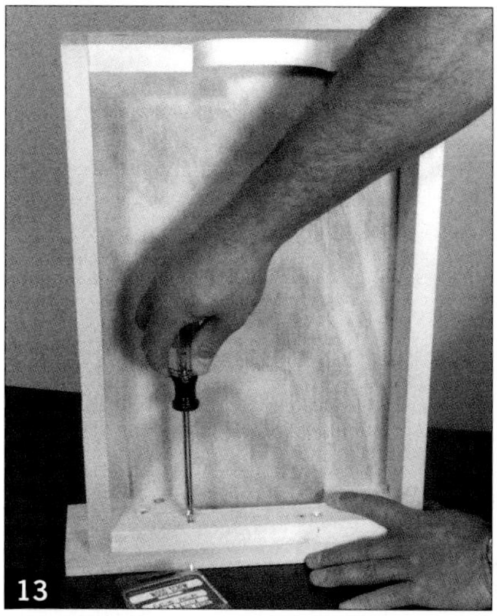

13 Place the drawer on top of the drawer face and fasten it with screws from inside to avoid marring the face.

14 Stain all of the outside surfaces. When dry, apply a clear finish such as the wiping finish (middle foreground) or a spray polyurethane (left foreground).

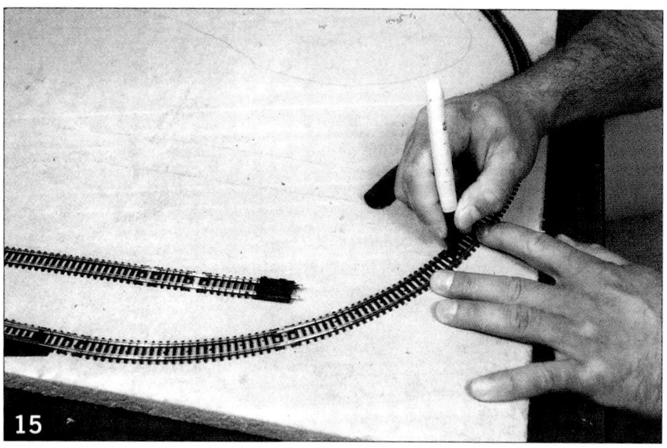

15 Temporarily assemble all of the track in its actual location on the Homasote while you're marking the center lines.

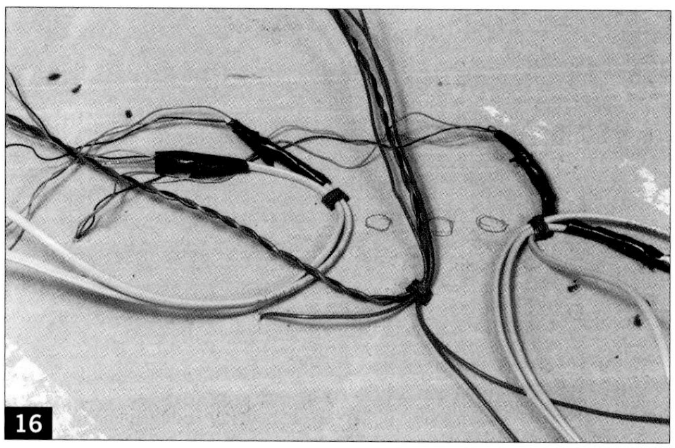

16 Here's the Homasote roadbed upside down. Mark locations of the wiring holes in the plywood. Secure the wires near the hole locations with insulated cable staples. The white diagonal marks are the locations of support blocks. Keep wires away from blocking.

After the scenery is completed, touch up the flat beige paint inside the box sides.

Acrylic cover

The cover for this layout is simply a rectangular piece of ⅜"-thick acrylic. My supplier recommended ½"acrylic for a table this size if you plan to place heavy objects on it, especially in the middle. Alternatively, you could support the thinner acrylic in the center with a block of wood disguised as a scenic feature.

You can have your supplier polish the edges (for a pretty penny) or you can sand them yourself as I did. I added self-adhesive plastic buttons under the acrylic just inside each corner of the box. This keeps the top centered on the layout box for a much neater appearance, **26**. Check online or in the Yellow Pages (under "plastics") for a supplier or dealer for acrylic. If

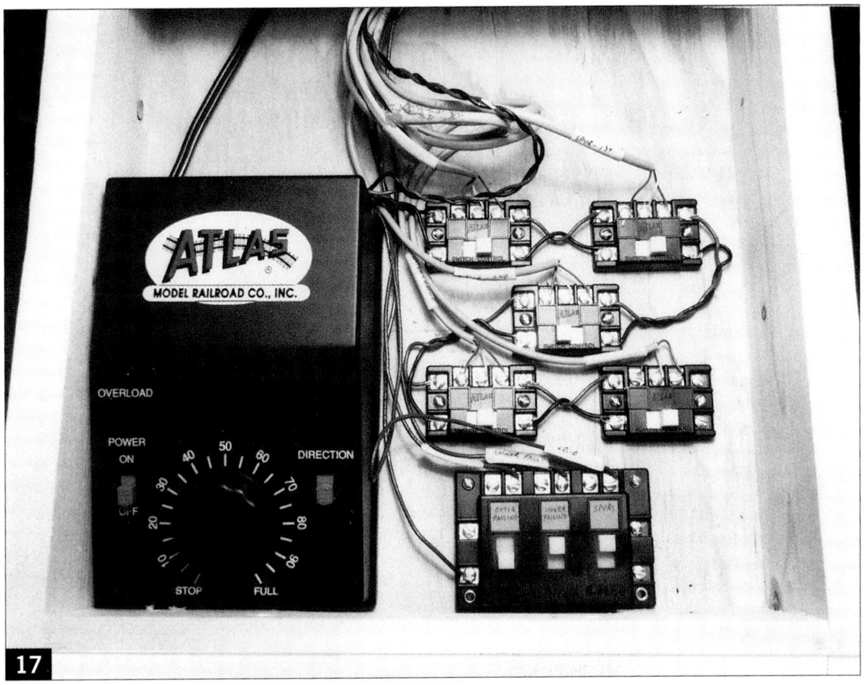

17

Install wiring controls as shown. The wires are bundled and tied (above). This bundle, and the power pack supply wire, may need to be coaxed into the drawer when closing it to help it slide all the way in. A little storage room is available in the rear of the drawer.

18

Operators have full control of block power and turnouts from the drawer. In order to access the interchange track or change rolling stock, remove the clear acrylic top.

19 Glue bridge abutment blocks under the bridge ends. You can see some support blocking under the Homasote to the right.

20 Stack pieces of broken ceiling tile and glue them together to form rock faces. Apply strips of 1½"-wide masking tape around the lake to support the Sculptamold.

21 The finished scene at Lake Brookeville looks quite tranquil.

22

Scenery stages, from the near right to the upper left: bare ceiling tile mountains, bare structure bases, structure bases with Sculptamold, lake banks made of Sculptamold, and ceiling tile rock face blended with Sculptamold.

Structure and scenery locations

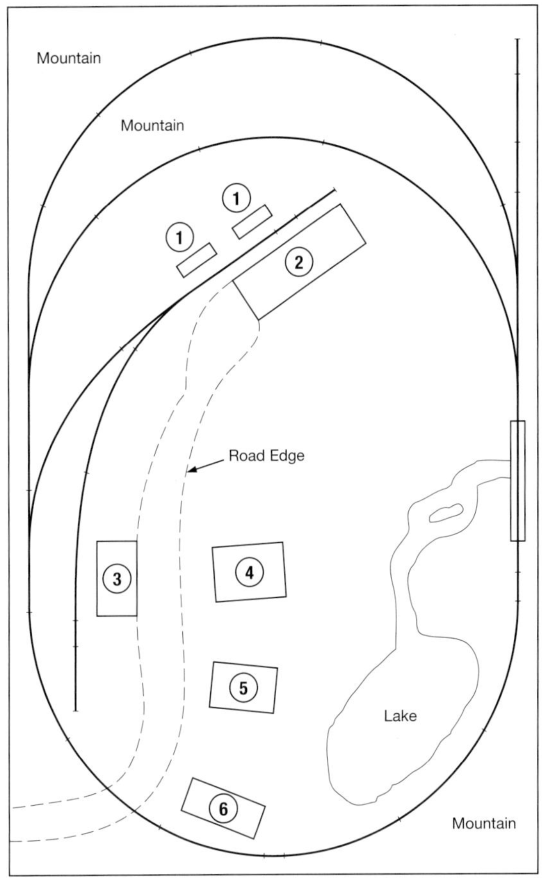

NO.	NAME	ORIGIN
1	Fuel Tanks	Walthers #3206
2	Brookeville Farm Supply	Lifelike #7444
3	Depot	Pola #208
4	Stores & Apartments	Lifelike #J7406
5	House	Model Power #1513
6	Passenger Platform	Bachmann #45906

23

you cannot find acrylic locally, a mail-order supplier is listed on the suppliers and manufacturers section.

Rolling stock

With standard curves, any ready-to-run rolling stock appropriate to the period you are modeling is fine. Once again, shorter locomotives and rolling stock will look better.

Most N scale rolling stock today already comes equipped with Micro-Trains or other magnetic couplers. Converting other cars to magnetic couplers for remote uncoupling is fairly easy, especially if you use the trucks with couplers attached. You simply swap them for the stock trucks and couplers. Cars with body-mounted couplers will be more difficult to uncouple because of the uncoupling magnets located on the curved tracks.

Most locomotives also already come equipped with knuckle couplers, which is good, because converting locomotives is more challenging than with rolling stock; some require modifications to the body. Micro-Trains has a comprehensive coupler guide book for this purpose.

Variations

- The trolley layout shown in Chapter 6 is approximately the same size if you prefer that type of layout.
- Include more rail spurs in the corners or at the bridge location. Again, you will sacrifice space for scenery.
- If you want a more traditional furniture look, legs in styles such as Shaker or Queen Anne's are available from Rockler, listed in the appendix.
- Substitute glass for the top if you want greater scratch resistance. The trade-off is a heavier weight.
- Expand the length of the layout to serve as a coffee table if you prefer this table design instead of the one in Chapter 4.
- Make a matching coffee table as well as one or two end tables for a set of model railroad furniture.
- Change the height of the table—this can be done simply by changing the lengths of the legs used. Typical end table heights vary between 19" and 31", with 26" being the standard.

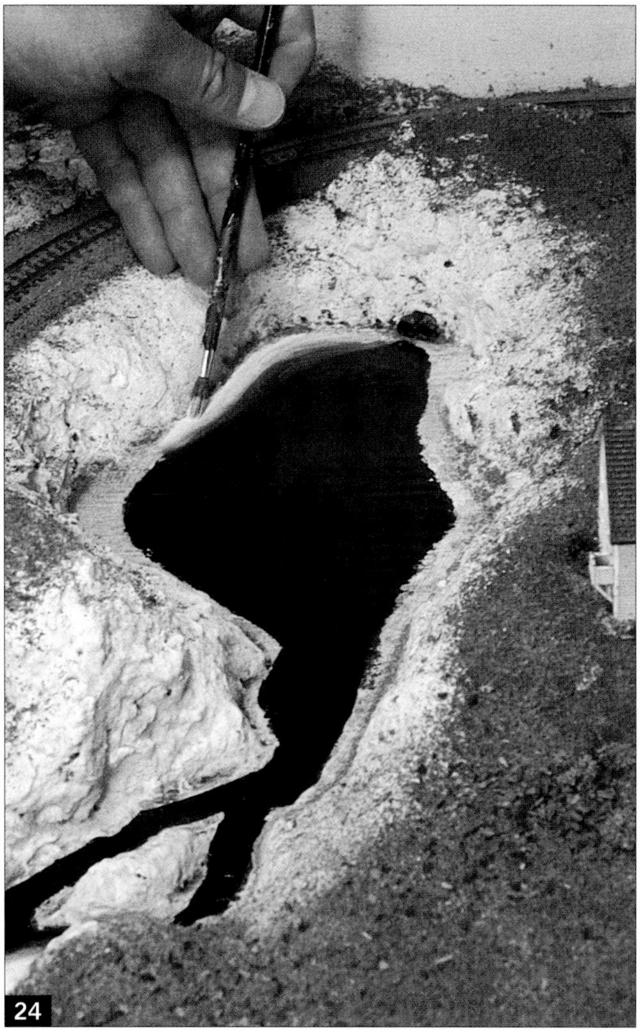

Paint the center of the lake with a flat black water-based hobby or craft paint. Immediately begin to feather in the same latex beige paint used for scenery around the edges to simulate shallow areas.

Pour the E-Z Water into the lake area after heating according to its instructions. The towel is protecting the finished box surfaces.

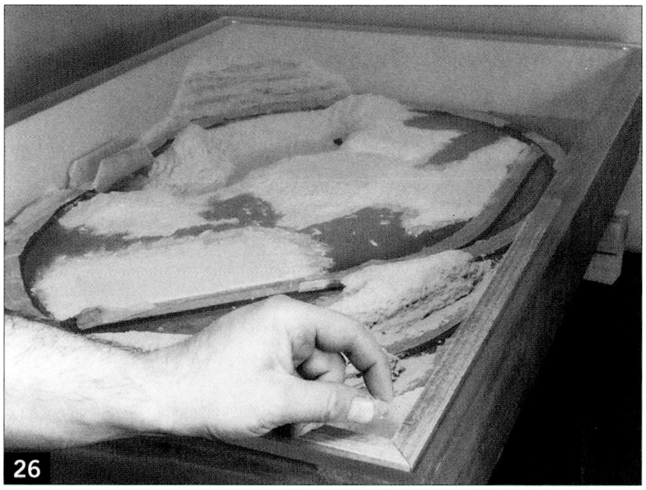

Lay the acrylic on top of the box. Place adhesive buttons so they will be just inside the box corners when the top is turned over.

Bill of materials

Lumber
- 1 x 6, 6' poplar boards, 2
- 1 x 4, 6' poplar board, 1
- 1 x 3, 6' No. 2 pine board, 1
- ½" plywood, 4' x 4' sheet
- ½" Homasote, 4' x 8' sheet
- ¾" square trim, 12'

Hardware
* No. 8 x 1" flathead wood screws or drywall screws
* No. 8 x 1¼" flathead wood screws or drywall screws
* 1¼" finishing nails
* 1" wire brads
- Emco no.WMT-114, round tapered 14" legs, mounting plates, and associated screws, 4 (substitute legs, mounting plates, and hardware from Waddell—see the suppliers and manufacturers section)
- Drawer handle

Track and wiring
- Atlas no. 2700 LH turnout, 3
- Atlas no. 2701 RH turnout, 2
- Atlas no. 2501 5" straight, 1 pkg.
- Atlas no. 2510 9¾" radius, 3 pkgs.
- Atlas no. 2532 rerailers, 1 pkg.
- Atlas no. 2536 bumpers, 1 pkg.
- Atlas no. 2546 Warren truss bridge
- Atlas no. 2509 track assortment
- Atlas no. 2540 track nails
- Atlas no. 311 power pack
- Atlas no. 2538 insulated joiners
- Atlas no. 205 connector
- 22-gauge stranded wire (single conductor), 20'
- 24-gauge stranded wire (three-conductor), 20'
- Magnetic uncouplers, Micro Trains no. 1310, 2 pkgs.
* Insulated cable staples
* Wire ties

Scenery
* Cellulose suspended ceiling tile
* Matte medium

27

A freight train rolls out from the rock cut. The rock formations work well as view blocks.

Bill of materials *(continued)*

- * Sculptamold
- • Woodland Scenics E-Z Water
- • Woodland Scenics ballast no. B75 (fine gray)
- * weeds for trees
- * ground foam, assorted

Structures

- • (substitutes indicated where structures no longer available)
- • Life-Like no. 7444 Merchant's Warehouse—substitute Atlas no. 2849 Maywood Station
- • Pola no. 208 goods depot—substitute Walthers Golden Valley freight house no. 2610
- • Walthers no. 3206 service track structures—substitute Walthers no. 3265 storage tanks
- • Life-Like no. J7406 general store—substitute Model Power no. 1539 post office and bank
- • Model Power no. 1513 farmhouse—substitute Atlas no. 2851 classic American home
- • Bachmann no. 45906 station platform

Miscellaneous

- * Minwax stain (golden oak)
- * Poly/oil satin finish
- * Wood primer
- * Flat latex beige, Sears no. 597
- * Craft paint, concrete color
- * Craft or hobby paint, silver
- * Craft or hobby paint, black
- * 1½" masking tape
- * electrical tape
- • Cork roadbed, 5
- * Wood glue
- • 3⁄16" foam core, 20" x 30" sheet
- • Drinking straw or styrene tube
- * 1⁄32" x 1⁄16" stripwood
- * Sandpaper
- * Tack cloth
- • 3⁄8" acrylic sheet, 25½" x 38½"

*Quantity as needed or desired

1

CHAPTER SIX

The Freedonia Transportation Authority

An N scale trolley layout on a rolling cart

The author's son Brian operates the layout, which is packed with details in only a 27" x 36" space. The cabinet below provides space for controls and storage.

The theme of this compact layout is a city scene with a trolley on a point-to-point track arrangement. An automatic reversing circuit provides hands-off display operation. This layout is designed for someone that prefers model construction more than operation and would like a nice setting to display their work, **1**.

The space advantage is provided by the rolling cabinet on which the layout is placed. Simply roll it to the corner of a room or into another room or closet when not in use, **2, 3.**

The kitbashed and scratchbuilt structures are for moderately advanced modelers, but you could easily substitute kit-built or factory-assembled buildings, especially if the angled road is made perpendicular to the others. Another unique feature of this chapter is the optional acrylic top that can be constructed to cover the layout.

Cabinet

I chose a kitchen utility cabinet as a base for this layout. The open shelf just under the top is an ideal place for a power pack and other controls you might need. The enclosed portion of the cabinet can be put to use for layout-related storage. Many similar cabinets are available in department stores or kitchen supply stores. Some have drawers that could hold the electrical controls as demonstrated in Chapters 3 and 5.

You could attach the layout permanently or semi-permanently to the cabinet with screws from below. This is a personal decision based on how frequently you would move the cabinet, whether you would like to transport the layout to places such as model shows or club meetings, and whether you want to leave the cabinet in its original condition.

2 The advantage of using a rolling cabinet to hold this layout is shown: it can be stored in a closet or brought out to be used with almost no set-up or break-down time. The acrylic top is very easy to construct and provides plenty of protection. Remember to account for the clear width of any opening through which the layout must pass.

Layout frame

Build the frame to support this layout from 1 x 3 lumber in an open-grid style with butt joints as shown in Chapters 2 and 3. The plans are on page 65. You could use 1 x 2 lumber if you do not need as much space as I did for the electrical accessories, **4, 5**.

Begin by cutting all the components to their sizes, **5, 6**. Before assembly, drill the holes for electrical accessories. I used a 1½" hole saw in an electric drill for the large holes in frame member A. You could also use a saber saw or do this manually with a coping saw. Appearance is not important if you cover the frame with paneling as outlined later.

Assemble the components with no. 8 x 1½" flathead wood screws and wood glue. Drill and countersink the screw holes to avoid splitting the wood, especially at the corner joints, **7**.

Next, cut a piece of ½" Homasote measuring 27" x 36". Mount it directly to the frame with the same size screws.

Track

The key to making this layout possible is the ability of flextrack to bend to a very tight radius and the ability of Homasote to securely hold track spikes. I drew the track plan and building outlines directly on the Homasote, **8**. After running the trolleys I had on some mock-ups, I settled on a minimum radius of 5" as a compromise between appearance and operation. I laid out the curves with easements as shown in Chapter 3.

Leave more clearance than normal on the inside of curves because of the greater overhang of locomotives and rolling stock. Test the equipment you have to be sure. I used an NMRA track gauge and added an extra ⅜" of clearance to the inside and ¼" of clearance to the outside of each curve.

Spike the flextrack in every spike hole provided. If you find it neces-

3

A streetcar rounds the corner by the Freedonia Police Station. Hopefully those demolition workers will stay out of the way. Weathered structures, details, and mini-scenes add up to a very realistic setting. The Daily Gibberish News is scratchbuilt; most other structures are kitbashed. The *Super Chief* is barreling through on a mock-up in front of the layout.

sary to keep the track flat on the tight curves, add additional spike holes with a no. 65 drill bit in a miniature drill (pin vise). Cut the flextrack, join it, and solder it at each joint as shown in Chapter 3, working outward from the crossing. If you choose a different track plan that requires insulated rail joiners, install them as you go.

One end of the line is disguised with a dummy (non-operating) turnout. Run one set of tracks right up to (but not touching) the other; create the second point rail with a small piece of rail glued to the ties. The other end of the line is a small maintenance yard with a short section of ballasted track.

Wiring

Wire the track as a single block. I soldered pairs of power wires in two different places as insurance against the need to dig up the streets in the future. Freedonia's road crews are a lazy bunch.

This layout contains quite a few electrical accessories, **4, 9**. I illuminated most of the buildings, provided many streetlights, and added commercial circuits for the automatic reversing feature and the flickering light inside the structure on fire.

You could theoretically gang all of the accessory wires together and solder away. However, this leaves you with a mess if anything needs to be repaired or replaced. Being optimistic is fine, but being realistic is just as important—things will go wrong or bulbs will burn out. Organizing wires on terminal strips will likely save hassles later.

Terminal strips provide screw connections for each wire; any single wire can be removed without affecting others. You can make your own simply by screwing bronze spring weather-stripping to the frame members, **10**. This material is used for weather-stripping doors and is available in hardware stores or home centers. Be sure to place the lower strip above the bottom edge of the frame members to prevent marring surfaces that the layout will sit on. Alternatively, you could purchase screw-type terminal strips from Radio Shack or other electrical suppliers.

Mount a pair of terminal strips on each of the three frame members C. No. 4 x ⅜" sheet-metal screws hold the strips in place and act as terminal screws. Drill holes in the terminal strips wherever you need them or poke through the strips with an awl to start screws. The ¼" holes shown between the terminal strips allow wires to pass through the frame members to reach the nearest pair of terminal strips.

Track plan

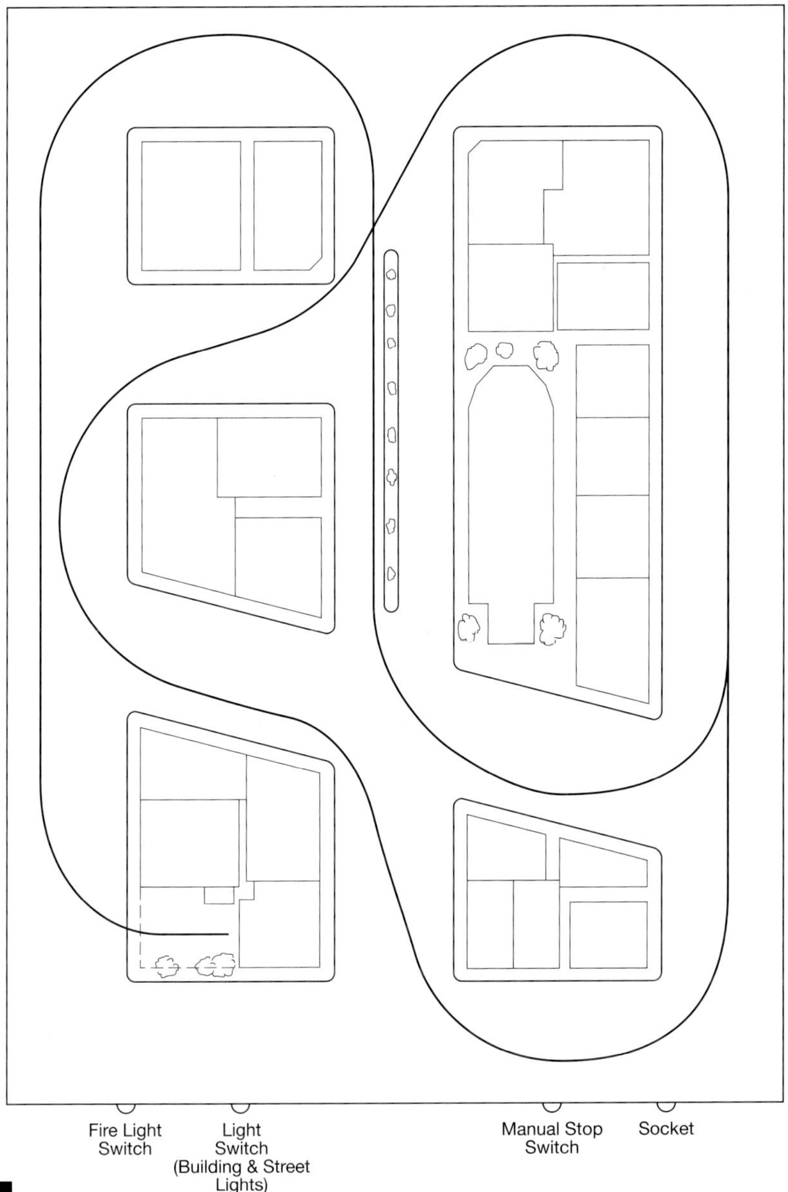

4

Install the Circuitron automatic reversing circuit and its power supply unit directly to the bottom of the Homasote and wire them as directed by the manufacturer. A number of manufacturers offer similar circuits. The one I chose has a manual stop feature, an adjustable time delay before reversing (which I thought was important for realism), and light sensitivity adjustments for each eye.

The electric eyes that stop the train at each end are included with the circuit. They are very unobtrusive; locate them between the rails near each end of the line. I bought a momentary action switch for the optional manual stop feature.

I used a matching electrical plug and socket set as a disconnect point for track and accessory wires coming from the power pack. Mount the socket on the front of the layout with the switches, **11**.

Now is the time to run lots of trains or trolleys and find and correct any problems before proceeding. This step cannot be over-emphasized on any layout, but it's especially important here. Making adjustments later will cause more damage than usual because of the streets and the structures.

To simplify replacing bulbs, install the building lights and the GRS Super Flamemaker for the building fire on ⅜" wooden dowels mounted on wood bases. One screw holds the base to the dowel and two screws attach the base to the layout. An insulated wire tie or rubber band holds the wires to the dowel under each light; the entire assembly fits through a ½" hole. Glue the streetlights in place with CA. Install these items as you construct the blocks of buildings. I wired the structure lamps and streetlights in series pairs to give a softer look and to save bulb life as shown in **9**.

At this time, add the paneling on the sides of the layout to improve its appearance. You could use tempered hardboard paneling sections (as I did), or any material you prefer. Cut it to fit the final dimensions and attach the pieces with screws so they can be removed if necessary. Since they're visible, I used brass screws for a nicer appearance. Before installing the side panel with the electric switches and jack, drill the appropriate holes and attach these items. Their bodies fit through the 1½" holes that you previously drilled in the frame.

Streets

I used a product called Scalecrete to pave the streets. This material is no longer available, but a close substitute is Scale Concrete from Scenic Express (see the manufacturers and suppliers section in the appendix). Work the material into the areas you need for street trackage; it results in a realistic texture. Alternatively, you could use the Atlas road system, joint compound, or Durham's Water Putty as in Chapter 5. Before paving, install pieces of ⅛" foam core under the areas where you will place the sidewalks and buildings.

I made two pavement-smoothing tools (**12**) to keep the level of the paving material below the tops of the rails. This is necessary so that you can use track cleaners later. The tools are made from readily available styrene sheet and strip materials.

Install .020" x .060" strip styrene "dams" to form flangeways (the space needed for the wheel flanges to ride

Layout frame, top view

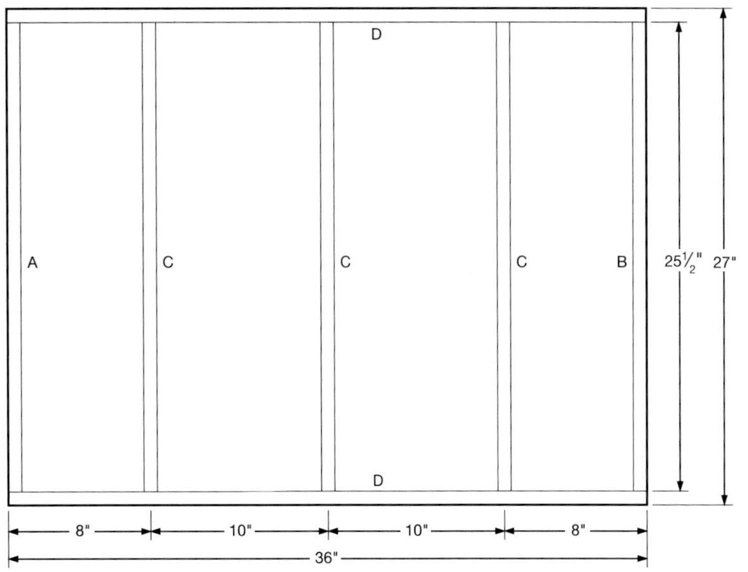

5

inside each rail). Paint these strips a concrete color to match what will be the final color of the streets. When the paint is dry, butt these strips upright against the inside of the spikes molded into the flextrack and glue them on with plastic solvent cement. The strips will provide the correct flangeway width without having to measure them, as long as the strip remains vertical. Hold the strip in place, run the solvent along the ties, hold for a few seconds, and move on.

Apply the paving material between these dams with a small flat screwdriver. Work on approximately 2" at a time and smooth the material with tool no. 1, **14**. Clean any stray material out of the flangeways as you go and clean the tool frequently.

Next, spread paving material outside the tracks right up to the rail with a

Cutting diagram

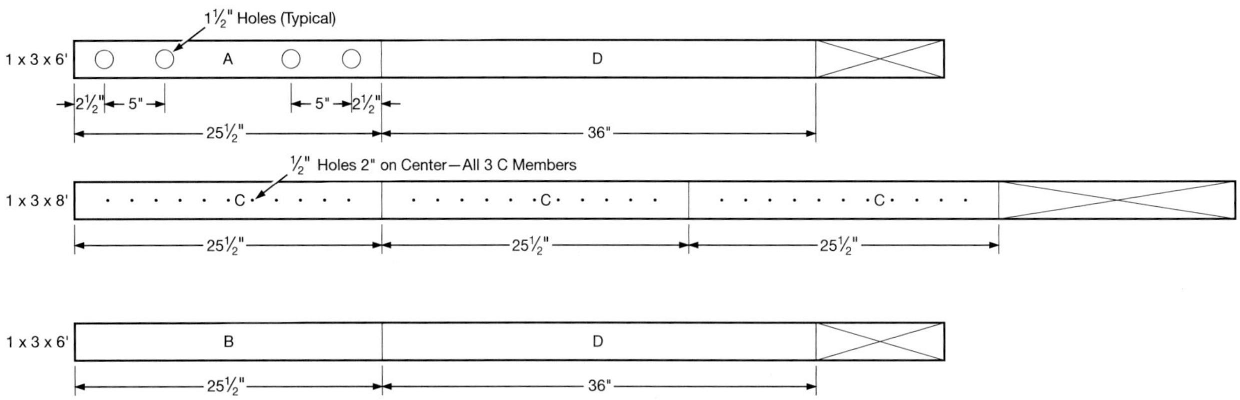

6

7

The frame goes together quickly and securely with screws. The large holes in the end piece were cut with the hole saw pictured just above the screwdriver.

8

To make an easement, offset the curve center line $\frac{1}{8}$" from the center line for the straight track. When the flextrack is laid, it will flow nicely from one to the other.

small putty knife. Smooth it out until you are satisfied with the appearance, then run tool no. 2 outside the rail, **15**. Dipping the putty knife and the smoothing tool in water sometimes helps the smoothing process.

When the roads are dry, score expansion joints and cracks with a hobby knife. Unpainted Scale Concrete resembles lightly weathered concrete. I painted my roads with a very diluted (about 1 part paint, 20 parts water) mix of black latex paint to look more weathered and highlight the cracks.

You may notice that I simulated old cobblestone showing through the pavement by installing pre-painted brick material before paving. I also simulated manholes by punching circles out of thin cardboard and pushing them into the wet paving material.

Finally, clean the rail heads with a track cleaner. Remove any stray material in the flangeways. Run trains again to troubleshoot any problems before you install structures.

Sidewalks, structures, and details

Plan groups of buildings for each block to determine the exact size of the blocks, **16**. Cut a sheet of .040"-thick styrene sheet material for each block, including the sidewalks. After cutting the sheets to size, score expansion joints and cracks with a hobby knife on all sidewalk and alley areas. Then, to simulate curbing, cement .040"-square styrene strips along the perimeter of each styrene sheet with styrene cement.

Wiring diagram

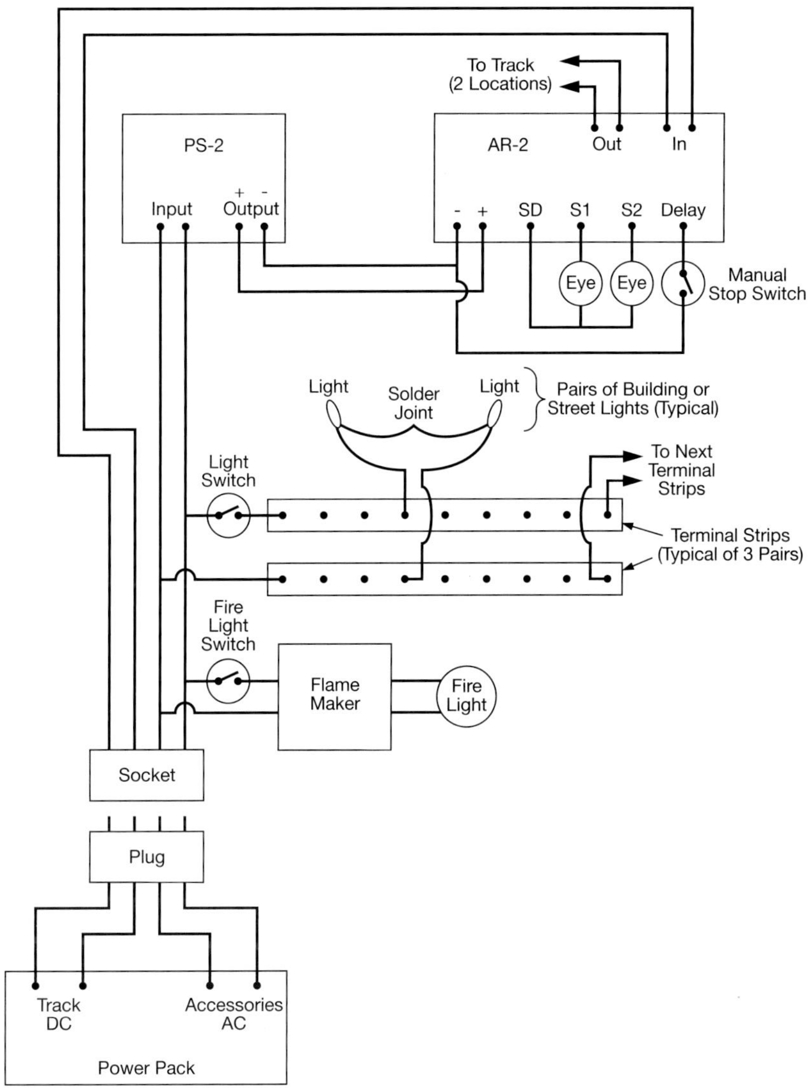

9

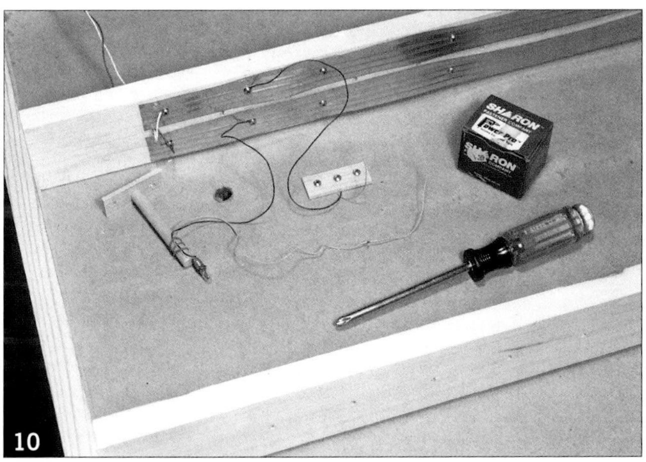

10

The terminal strips are made from weather stripping. They allow removal of any single wire if needed. Lights for structures are mounted on removable dowels with bases.

11

A four-conductor socket and plug allows wires from the power pack (two for accessories, two for track power) to be easily connected.

Paving tools (all pieces are styrene)

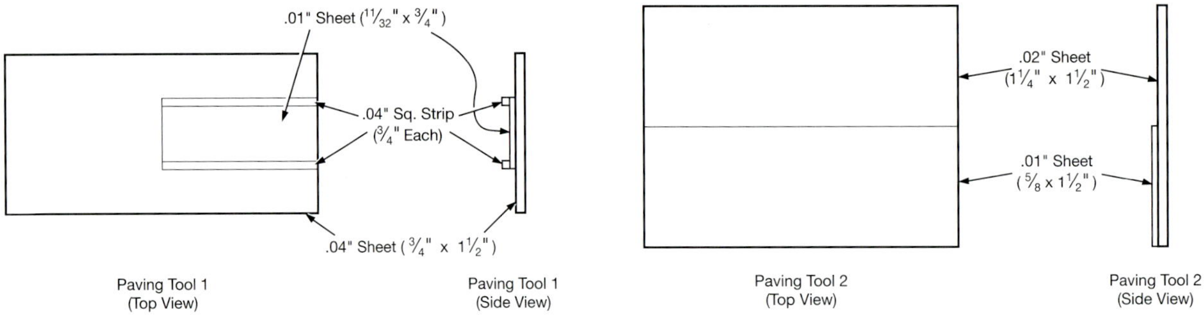

12

13

A patrol car turns the corner by the bar as a streetcar heads the other way.

14

After mounting styrene dams to form flangeways, the paving material is placed in the center and smoothed with paving tool no. 1.

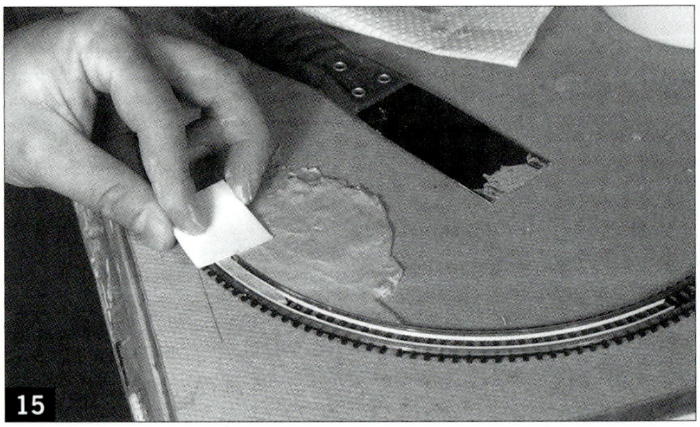

15

Spread the material outside the track and smooth it with paving tool no. 2. This will keep the material below the tops of the rails.

Paint each assembly (I used Model Master light gray). Then weather each assembly with powdered black chalk to highlight the joints and cracks. Install the assemblies with Walther's Goo. When dry, drill the holes for lights through the styrene and Homasote. See the photos of finished scenes for the final appearance of the sidewalks.

Build the structures together in blocks to ensure that they fit together. To achieve the look I wanted, I did extensive kitbashing (modifying stock kits). I shortened walls, angled others, and used plain styrene for walls that would not show, **17**. I also exchanged parts between kits and added many details. The result is a layout that has mostly unique structures. For more information on kitbashing, refer to Art Curren's *Kitbashing HO Model Railroad Structures* (Kalmbach). Although it's now out of print, you can still find copies online or through dealers.

You could opt for more stock structures, especially if you choose not to have an angled street. Another idea would be to have more alleys where the buildings do not fit together exactly. These provide a place for many details to add interest for viewers.

If you are so inclined, you could scratchbuild many structures. I scratchbuilt two structures on this layout, and it was fun (see articles in the April and December 1995 issues of *Model Railroader*). I intentionally made the structures difficult because I wanted this project to last for a few years during a time when I had very little modeling space. Exercise your imagination and choose the structures you desire.

I gave many of the structures humorous names. The viewer who goes to the trouble of reading the tiny sign "Dewey, Cheatum, and Howe, Attorneys-at-Law" or "Bill M. Dailey Collection Agency" deserves the chuckle he or she will get. This is a great way to maintain interest. I made many of these signs using my home computer and printer. Others are dry transfer lettering which is simply rubbed on.

Another method to maintain interest is to use mini-scenes. These also help to break up the layout and make

16

Sidewalks are scored sheet styrene with strip styrene curbs.

17

Here's a top view of the layout with half of the structures in place. You can vary the angles of the streets and the exact track location based on your choices of structures.

18

The pedestrian better watch carefully for both rail and road traffic. The lady in the second floor window is about to drop a pot on her husband's head if he doesn't leave the card game below. Sam Buca's Beer and Brawl is scratchbuilt.

it seem larger. I used a structure on fire, a car wreck, a car fire, a wedding in progress, a utility work scene, a building under construction, sidewalk demolition, a building under demolition, a sidewalk card game outside of a bar, **18**, and a busy movie theater.

I made the trees as shown in Chapter 2. I also included a large number of detail parts, both homemade and commercial. I kitbashed some of the vehicles, including most fire trucks.

Acrylic cover

Providing an acrylic cover over the layout has several advantages as outlined in the introduction. If the cover is strictly for storage, it can be a wooden box. If you want to view the layout with the cover on, you'll have to make the lid of a clear material. Here I will show the construction of a five-sided acrylic cover.

A large plastics supplier will have the acrylic, cement, and cement applicator. If you have trouble locating a supplier, Piedmont Plastics, listed in the suppliers and manufacturers section, will take online orders. I found it cost-effective and handy to have my supplier cut the pieces to size. This is because they only charged for the exact size pieces after cutting. This is not always the case, so price it both ways if you have the ability to cut the material.

My supplier suggested that I use at least ¼"-thick acrylic for this size project. Thicker material would provide stronger joints, but I decided to use 3⁄16" panels to balance strength versus weight. I wanted the top to be easily removable—remember reality! The cover has proved to be durable if it is removed and replaced carefully.

The first step in assembly is to attach all five sections of the cover with masking tape, **19**. Position joints as in **20** for cementing. Lay the assembly on the correct side to cement two of the corner joints. Wait a few minutes for the cement to set, then turn the assembly on the opposite side. After checking positioning, cement the two other side joints. Finally, turn the assembly upside down and cement all four side/top joints.

The solvent cement used for these joints requires a special applicator and procedure, although the technique is easy to learn. Fill the applicator bottle half-way with cement. Squeeze the bottle to remove most of the air, **21**. Turn the bottle over while releasing pressure so that air is entering, preventing cement from pouring out where you do not want it. Quickly position the applicator tip over one end of the joint and run it along the entire joint while squeezing out cement, **22**. Try it a few times and you will get the hang of it. What you see is my first try; it was easy. I found out later that joints can be re-cemented easily if they ever come apart. Since any spilled cement will mar the panels, I suggest laying rags over them to catch any spills.

By this time I am sure that you realize the acrylic cover needs something to sit on, or your precious structures will be crushed. For this I built a tray of ½" plywood and 1 x 2 lumber with glue and nails, **23**, **24**. Drill a hole

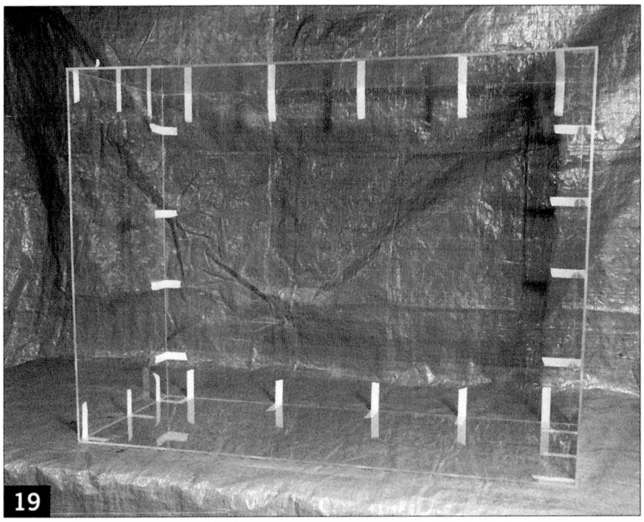

19

Assemble the acrylic panels temporarily with masking tape.

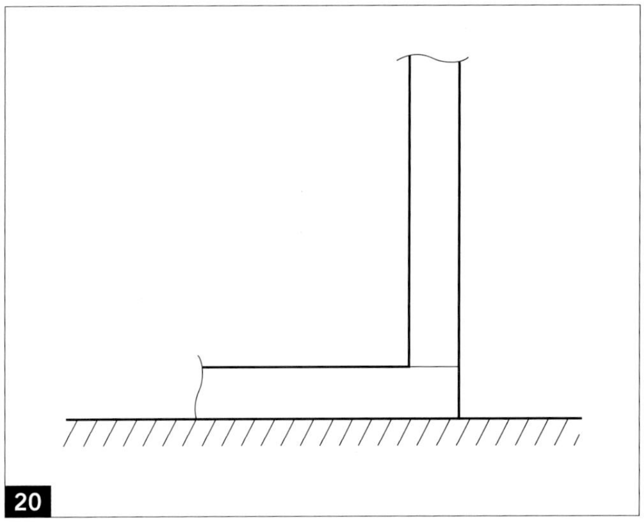

20

The acrylic joints must be oriented as shown to be cemented.

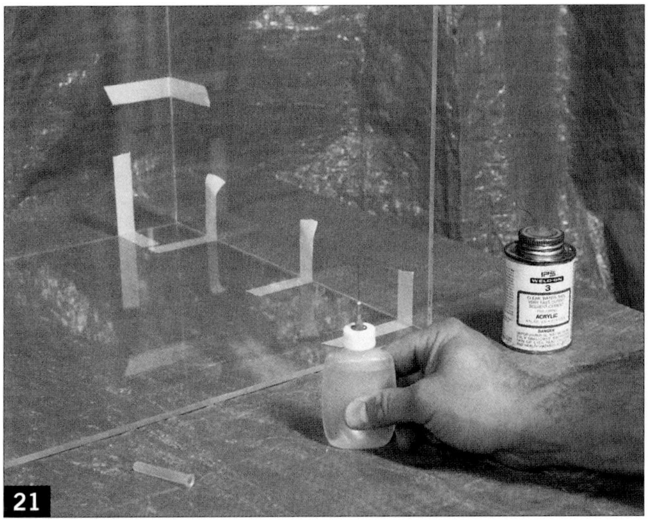

21

After filling the applicator bottle half-way with cement, most of the air is squeezed out. Be sure not to point the applicator at the assembled top in case a drop accidentally comes out.

22

Immediately after releasing the pressure on the bottle, turn it over and position it on one end of the joint while air enters the tip. Squeeze out cement along the length of the joint.

Tray for acrylic cover

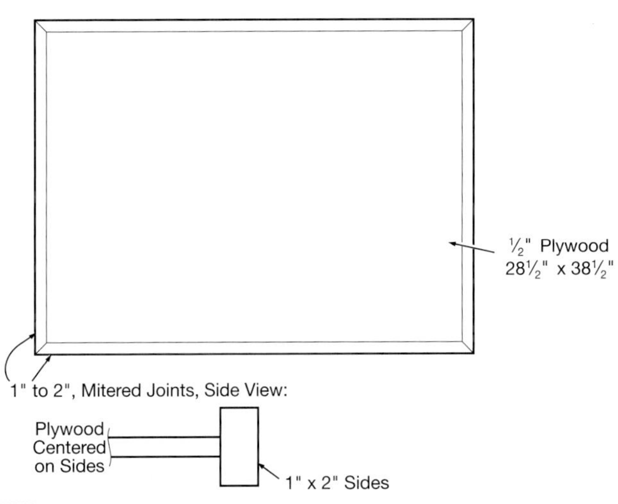

23

24

Assemble the tray with glue and nails.

Bill of materials (excluding rolling cabinet)

Layout lumber
- 1 x 3, 6' white pine, 2
- 1 x 3, 8' white pine, 1
- ½" Homosote 27" x 36"

* ⅜" dowels and scrap strips for light posts
* Paneling or tempered hardboard to cover edges

Tray lumber
- 1 x 2, 6' white pine, 2
- ½" plywood, 38½" x 28½"

Hardware
* Flathead wood screws, no. 8 x 1½", or 1¼" drywall screws
* Panhead sheet-metal screws, no. 4 x ⅜"
* 1¼" nails or brads
* Roundhead brass wood screws, no. 6 x ¾"
* Bronze spring weather-stripping for terminal strips

Electrical
- MRC Tech II Power Pack (Railpower 1300)
- Automatic Reversing Circuit, Circuitron AR-2
- Power Supply, Circuitron PS-2
- GRS Micro-Lighting Flamemaker
- Street lights, Model Power, 12
- Building lights, Model Power, 18
- Plug w/leads, Radio Shack no. 270-041A
- Socket w/leads, Radio Shack no. 274-1215
- Momentary switch, Radio Shack no. 275-618
- SPST push switches, Radio Shack no. 275-617, 2

* 22-gauge wire for power and accessory leads

Track (Atlas)
- No. 2568 30-degree crossing
- No. 2500 flextrack, 7
- No. 2535 rail joiners, 1 pkg.
- No. 2540 track nails, 1 pkg.

Scenery
- Scale Concrete or Atlas road system, 2 containers
- ⅛" foam core, 20" x 30"

* .040" styrene for sidewalks
* .040"-square strip styrene for curbs
* Styrene sheet for paving tools

- Ballast, Woodland Scenics no. B73, fine buff

* Weeds for trees
* Ground foam, assorted

Structures
- Vollmer no. 7760 cathedral
- Vollmer no. 7651 bank
- Model Power kits nos. 1540, 2584, 2607
- Faller kits nos. 232262, 232266, 232272, 232305, 232307
- Design Preservation Models kits nos. 50100 and 50200

Paint
* Model Master light gray no. FS36495 or gray craft paint
* Stain and clear finish (or paint) for tray

Acrylic sheet
- 3⁄16" panels, 28" x 15", 2
- 3⁄16" panels, 38⅜" x 15", 2
- 3⁄16" panel, 38⅜" x 28⅜"

* Solvent cement

- Cement applicator bottle

Miscellaneous
* Matte medium
* Wood glue

* Quantity as needed or desired

through the plywood near the connector to allow it to pass through the tray inside the cover. Either paint the tray or stain and varnish it. Place or mount it on the rolling cabinet, and then place the layout and cover on the tray. You might also consider building a lip into the layout frame to hold the top instead of making a separate tray.

Setup and rolling stock

I operate ready-to run trolleys from Bachmann and Model Power on my layout, **25**. I also kitbashed a trolley and a railcar using Arnold switcher chassis as bases.

Believe it or not, small locomotives and short rolling stock (with a 40' maximum length) will negotiate these 5" curves, especially if they have truck-mounted couplers. The lengths of the locomotives and rolling stock should be as consistent as possible, **26**.

To help keep the rails clean around all the detail contained in this layout, I invested in a Centerline Products rail cleaner. This runs along the layout, pushed or pulled by a locomotive or trolley, and works extremely well. The cleaning pad that is wound around the rolling drum needs to glued with a little Walthers Goo to work in both directions without unraveling.

In the background of many photos, you can see where I placed Radical Flats photo flats from King Mill Enterprises (see the suppliers and manufacturers section in the appendix). These are actual building photos printed on heavy cardstock. They have many uses on layouts, and are available in multiple scales.

Variations

- If you want more operating possibilities, include some spurs for switching.
- Consider an interchange track such as shown in Chapter 5.
- If you don't care for the city/trolley theme, a continuous-run layout such as the one in Chapter 5 will fit in approximately the same space.
- Moderately skilled woodworkers could build a custom cabinet. The obvious advantage to this would be to make it exactly the size you need and include the best type of storage for your materials, rolling stock, etc. Install casters as shown in Chapter 3.

25

More mini-scenes in Freedonia include a building under construction and opening night at the movie theater.

26

It looks like the wedding in front of the church has been interrupted by the passing railcar. Up the street you can see some background photo flats from the King Mill Enterprises Radical Flats line.

1

CHAPTER SEVEN

Coal River & Southern

An ultra-lightweight sectional O scale shelf layout

The compact L-shaped Coal River & Southern layout rests on wall-mounted brackets in the corner of a room. Similar techniques can be applied to layouts in almost any scale.

This railroad represents a short line serving a single on-layout industry and connecting with an off-layout main line, **1**. Jeff Peck, who did the trackwork, scenery, and structures for this layout, was inspired by the Coal River area of southern West Virginia. Like the Norwest Terminal layout in Chapter 2, this project is for those who prefer switching operation rather than continuous running. Many modelers may not think of a scale as large as O when small space comes to mind, however large scales permit a great deal of detailing—a good fit for those who like to build and detail structures and rolling stock.

2

A locomotive shoves a hopper car under the coal loader. That brand-new pickup truck won't stay shiny for long in coal country.

The space-saving concept illustrated here is mounting of the layout on wall brackets like a shelf. This allows the space below it to be put to use, taking no area from your living space. Both straight sections of this layout have removable legs to allow the layout to be set up and clamped together in other locations, such as a public show or a friend's house. Since the layout will be supported by wall brackets, the scenery is lightweight, **2**.

The layout frame is built as three interconnected sections, which allows portability, variability, and expandability. This is called "sectional" construction—the sections are meant to be connected in one or more specific ways. This is different than modular construction (such as Ntrak) where the modules have track in standard locations at their ends to allow the modules to be connected in any order.

This layout uses Digital Command Control (DCC). Power is still fed through the rails; however, decoders in locomotives allow them to be controlled independently without dividing the track into separate electrical blocks.

Straight frames and backdrops

The frames are similar to the Ntrak module in Chapter 3; however, they are lighter because they use ¼" plywood for the long sides and eliminate the plywood under the foam, **3**, **4**, **5**. This lightens the load on the shelf while still allowing portability. If the sections will be moved frequently, I would suggest using the plywood under the foam (see Chapter 3).

Follow the cutting diagrams (**4** through **7**) and cut members A, B, and C to size. Fasten the plywood sides A to ends B with wood glue and 1" drywall screws or no. 8 x ¾" flathead wood screws. Cut a 1" foam piece to fit within the frame—you can use the frame as a cutting guide.

Add cross-members C the same way, but be sure they are positioned 1" below the top of the frame to allow room for the foam subroadbed and scenery base. I find it easy to do this with the frame upside down and the foam placed in temporarily as a spacer—refer back to Chapter 3. Repeat this process to make a second straight frame.

Track plan

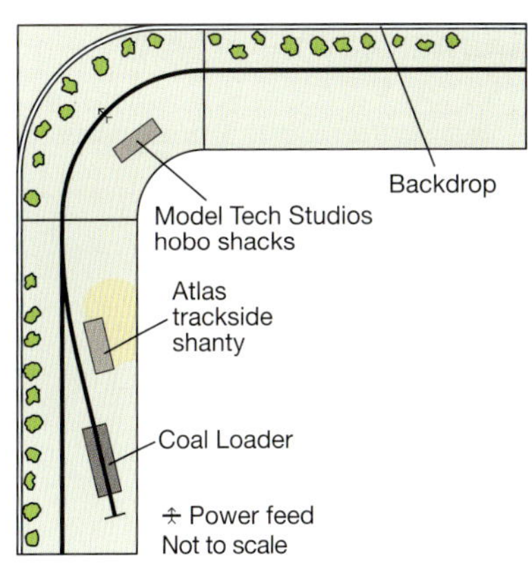

3

Straight layout frames

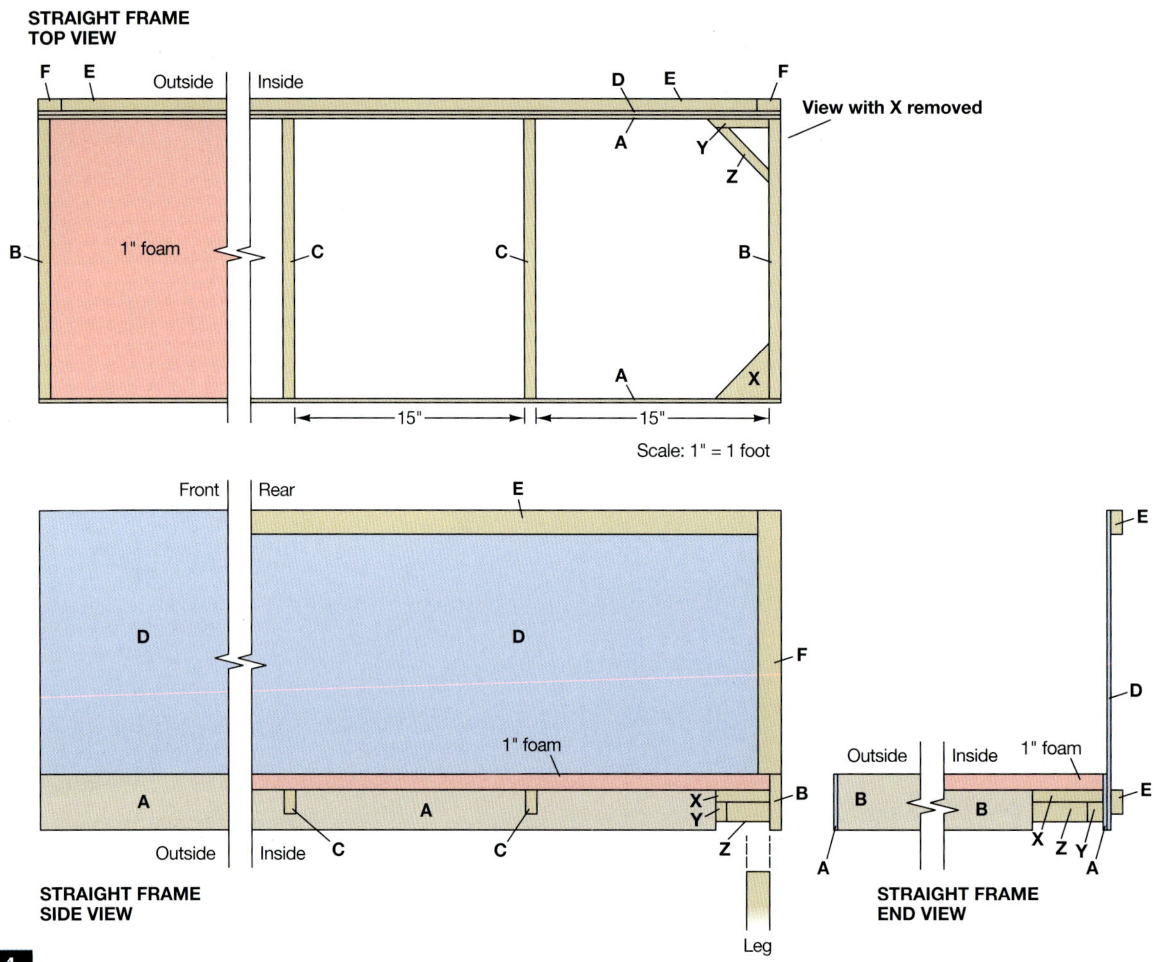

4

Corner Layout Frame

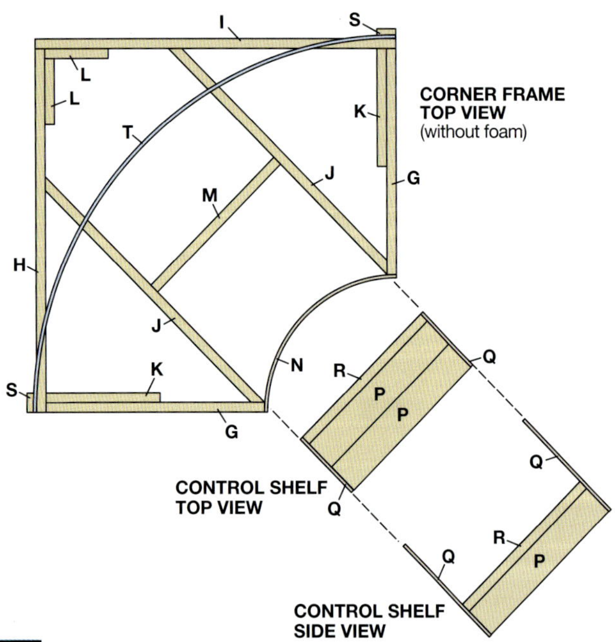

5

Brackets

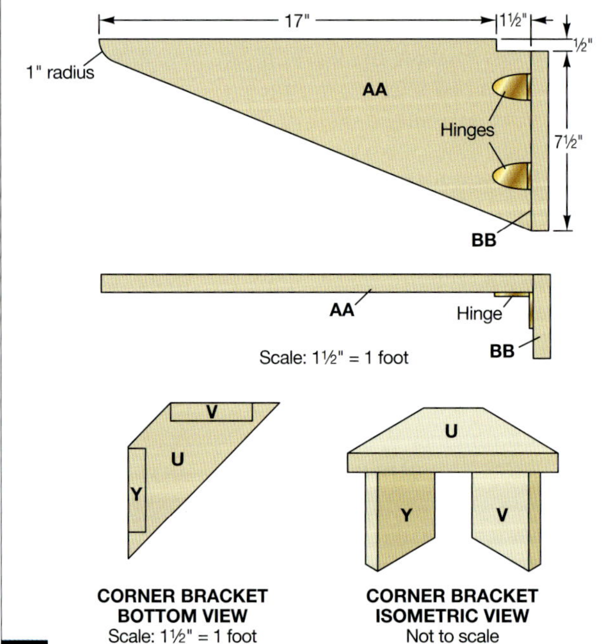

6

Cutting diagrams

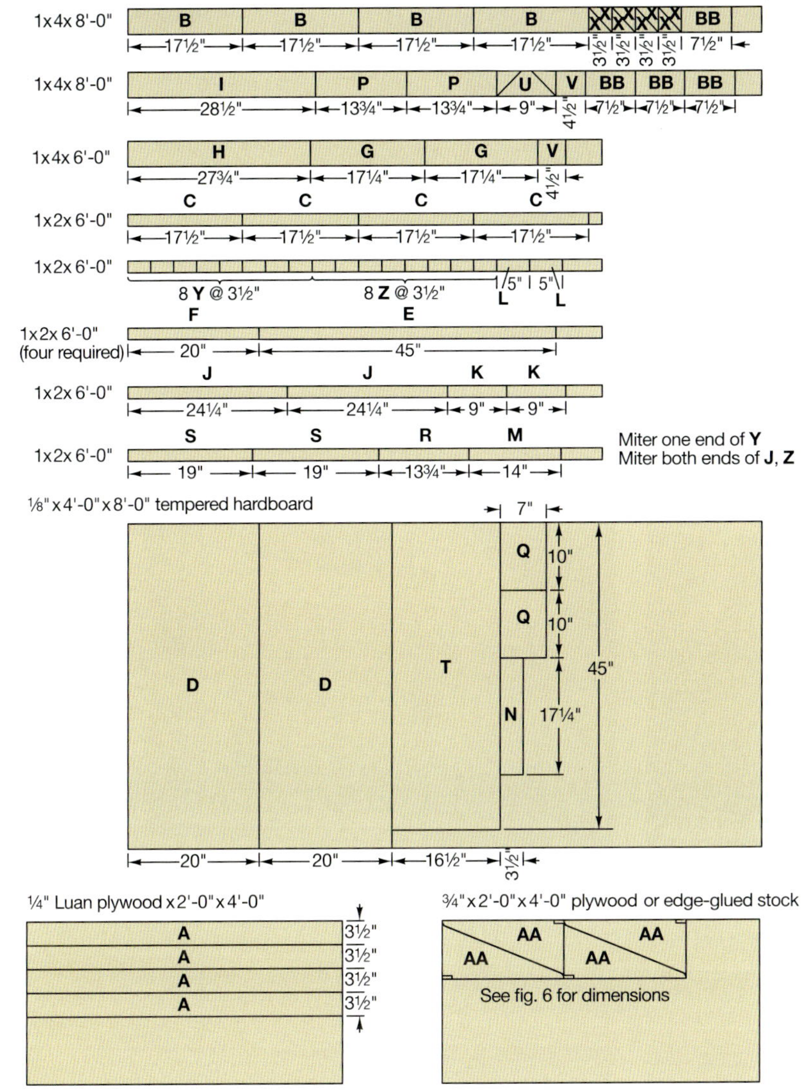

7

For the backdrop, cut members D, E, and F. Strengthen the perimeter of hardboard member D by fastening members E and F with no. 8 x ¾" flathead wood screws and wood glue. Then fasten the backdrop assembly to the frame with 3⁄16" x 2" machine bolts, washers, and wing nuts, **8**.

Legs and leg pockets

If you'd like the layout to remain on the wall brackets, you may skip this section—but then add blocking to side members B to support the foam subroadbed.

Fashion the triangular leg pockets with the frame upside down and the foam temporarily in place. Cut members X, Y, and Z. Keep the frame square while installing the leg pockets, especially the first one in each frame. A corner clamp or someone holding a square can be a great help. Fasten leg pocket top X to the frame sides and ends with wood glue and 1¼" drywall screws from the outside while holding the pocket top down against the foam. Fasten leg pocket side Y to the plywood frame side with wood glue and screws from the outside, **9**. Use ¾" or 1" screws through front member A and 1¼" screws through side member B.

Prepare the angled leg pocket member Z by first installing the insert nut which will hold the leg-retainer thumb screw. Drill a hole (sized per the instructions) through the center of member Z. From what will be the

8

One of the straight backdrops has been installed. You can see the bracing used on the rear.

9

With the frame upside down and the foam in place as a spacer, install the leg pocket parts. Member X is in place, Y is being fastened, and Z is awaiting installation.

10 I used an allen wrench to add the insert nut into the angled side Z of the leg pocket. Continue until it is flush with the wood surface.

11 Adding the angled piece completes the leg pocket.

12 Leg assembly, from right to left: (1) EMT conduit, (2) EMT with dowel inserted, (3) after drilling the dowel to accept the insert nuts and the nails partly driven through the EMT into the dowel, (4) the insert nut partly turned into the dowel, (5) the insert nut fully installed, and (6) the leg bolt installed.

13 Here's the finished leg pocket with a conduit leg in place. The thumb screw holds the leg in position.

14 Start the corner frame with the two corner pieces. The brace on top is temporary; it keeps the joint square.

15 While fastening the angled support member J, the 1" foam spacers keep the support at the proper height.

inside surface of the leg pocket, turn the insert nut into this hole with an Allen wrench, **10**. You can also use tee nuts for this as shown in Chapter 3. Complete the pocket by fastening member Z to member Y and frame end B with wood glue and 1¼" drywall screws from the inside, **11**. Repeat this to make seven more leg pockets—one in each corner of both straight frames.

Make the legs with ¾" electrical metallic tubing (EMT), a rigid conduit that is used for wiring, **12**. Cut eight pieces of EMT 36½" long. This will place the track height at 40" above the floor; you may adjust this as you prefer.

Cut eight pieces of ⅝" dowel to a length of 6". Slide a section of dowel

16

Continue the assembly of the corner frame. Leave the temporary brace in place on the top.

17

Install the cross member M between members J.

18

Clamp the curved front in place while fastening. The blocking (K and L) and the backdrop supports (S) are already in place.

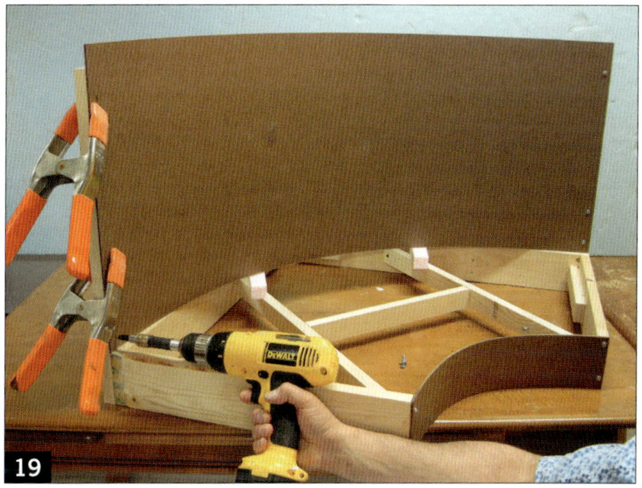

19

Install the corner backdrop. Notice the 1" spacers between it and the frame cross members J.

into one end of each EMT leg—tap it in if it is snug. The dowels may need to be sanded a bit thinner to fit.

Fix the dowels in place by drilling ¹⁄₁₆" holes through the EMT about 4" and 5" from the end. Don't drill too deeply into the dowel. Drive ⅝" brads through these holes into the dowels.

Drill a ⅜" hole about 3" deep into the end of each dowel. This hole must be as straight as possible. Clear all sawdust from the hole. Turn the threaded insert nuts into the dowels and screw the 3" carriage bolts all the way through the nuts. If they bind, remove the insert nut and carefully widen the hole with the same drill bit. Reinstall the insert nut and check again. Eye bolts or thumb screws turned into the insert nuts in the leg pockets hold the finished legs in the leg pockets, **13**.

Corner frame, curved backdrop

Cut members G, H, I, and J. Fasten rear member H to end member G using 1¼" drywall screws and wood glue. Keep the members square, **14**. With 1" foam spacers to account for the foam subroadbed, fasten angled cross member J to the H/G assembly, **15**, using screws and glue. Assemble the other side of the frame in the same manner with members G, I, and J.

Fasten the G/H/J assembly to the G/I/J assembly with screws and glue, **16**. After carefully checking the alignment of the entire frame assembly, measure between members J and cut member M to fit. Fasten member M with screws and glue, **17**.

Now cut members K, L, and S. Mount members K and L 1" below the top of the frame, using screws and glue, to serve as blocking under the 1" foam subroadbed. Fasten members S to the rear of the frame to support the curved backdrop. Use three screws and glue for each, **18**.

Cut members N and T from ⅛" tempered hardboard for the curved backdrop and front of the frame. Fasten member N to frame members G, **18**, with no. 8 x ¾" sheet-metal or roundhead wood screws. Clamps or a helper are a must.

Next, fasten backdrop member T to supports S, **19**. Use the same type of screws—two on each side low enough to be covered by scenery later, and one toward the top of the backdrop on each side. Once the backdrop is done, remove it temporarily. Use the corner frame itself as a cutting diagram for the foam subroadbed.

20

Assemble the shelf for the control unit.

21

Mount the control unit shelf to the corner section.

22

The straight frames are clamped together on their legs, with the foam and roadbed in place. The track is being installed.

23

Clear caulk secures the cork roadbed as well as the track. Don't apply the caulk near the throw bar of the turnout.

24

Removable track pieces bridge the gaps between layout sections.

25

The DCC station rests on its shelf below the corner section.

For the shelf that holds the DCC command station underneath the corner section, cut members P, Q, and R. Fasten members Q to members P, using wood glue and no. 8 x ¾" sheet-metal or roundhead wood screws. Fasten member R to the P/Q assembly, **20**. Finally, fasten the shelf assembly to frame members J using the same type of screws, **21**.

Trackwork

Secure the foam subroadbed to all three frames with foam-compatible construction adhesive. Weight it down to hold it while it dries. Also run a bead of adhesive between the foam and frame as shown back in **3-10**.

After marking the track location, glue the cork roadbed to the foam with construction adhesive or clear caulk (**22, 23**). The Kwik Seal Plus caulk shown grabs fast. Glue the track to the roadbed in the same way. Be careful near moving turnout parts. Pins or weights will hold curved track and roadbed while the adhesive dries.

Run the roadbed up to the mating edges of the sections. When laying track, leave a space for a removable connector track, **24**.

The sequence for the low-relief mountains is shown (left to right): bare vertical foam, plaster gauze, and black base coat of paint.

There is very little room for a person between the train and the hill. He had better find a safe spot as the train rolls past.

Install the hinges on the wall brackets.

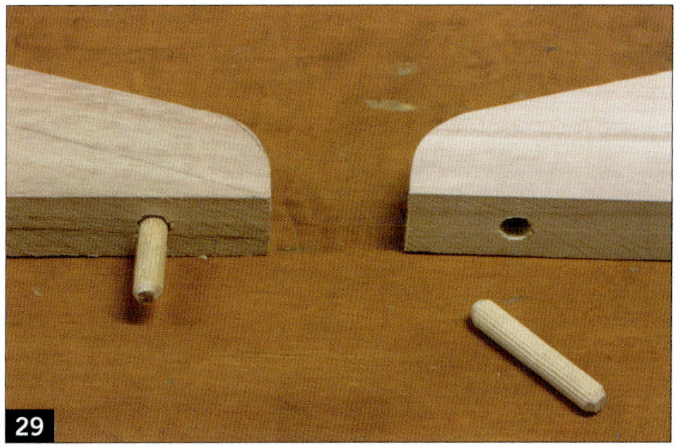

Dowels in the wall brackets will hold the layout sections in place, keeping them from sliding off the brackets.

Here's the completed corner bracket.

Install the wall brackets. Make sure the screws go into studs.

Wiring and controls

Place the Digitrax Zephyr command station/throttle on the shelf, **25**. Follow the Digitrax wiring directions and run two wires to the rails in the corner through a small terminal strip mounted under the corner frame. This will allow you to remove the control unit for transport. A plug-type connecter would also work.

Wire connectors should not be needed between layout sections, given the robustness of the O scale rail joiners. If you extend the layout to more sections and desire connectors, refer back to Chapter 3.

Scenery and structures

Decide if the backdrops on the straight frame sections will be removable before starting scenery. The corner backdrop must remain in place. Apply wood primer to the backdrops and frames.

Make low-relief hills where desired on one or both sides of the track by mounting extruded foam pieces vertically, **26**. Use plaster-impregnated gauze to form the hill contours.

Most rock faces were created by chipping the extruded foam as shown

Here's the corner bracket below the layout.

Modeler and builder Jeff Peck and his son Christian operate the Coal River & Southern.

Bill of materials

Lumber
- ¼" lauan plywood, 2' x 4'
- ⅛" tempered hardboard, 4' x 8'
- ¾" plywood, 2' x 4', or edge-glued stock at least 18" x 40"
- 1 x 4, 8' pine, 2
- 1 x 4, 6' pine, 1
- 1 x 2, 6' pine, 8
- ⅝" dowel, 4'
- ¼" dowel, 1' (or 4 dowel pins)

Hardware
- ¾" EMT (electrical metallic tubing), 3 10' lengths
- * 1" and 1¼" drywall screws
- * ⅝" brads
- ¼" threaded insert nuts, 16
- ¼" x 3" carriage bolts (to match insert nuts), 8
- ¼" x 2" thumb screws or eye bolts (to match insert nuts), 8
- * No. 8 x ¾" sheet-metal or roundhead wood screws
- * No. 8 x ¾" flathead wood screws
- 3⁄16" x 2" flathead machine bolts, washers, and wing nuts, 6
- Hinges, 8

Track and roadbed
- Atlas no. 7024 LH no. 5 turnout, 1
- Atlas no. 7056 flextrack, 6
- Midwest Products cork roadbed, 6

Electrical
- Digitrax Zephyr DCC command station/throttle
- 12-guage two-conductor wire, 2'
- Terminal strip

Scenery
- * Woodland Scenics plaster-impregnated gauze
- * Ground foam, trees
- * Scenic Express lightweight rock castings
- * Durham's Water Putty
- * Real rocks

Structures
- Atlas no. 6903 O scale trackside shanty
- Model Tech Studios no. OD2517P Hobo Shacks
- * Materials to scratchbuild the coal loader, including Radical Flats from King Enterprises

Miscellaneous
- 1" extruded foam insulation board, 4' x 8' sheet (for baseboard)
- 2" extruded foam insulation board, 2' x 8' sheet (for hill forms)
- * Wood glue
- * Wood primer
- * Flat sky blue paint
- * Flat black paint
- * Semi-gloss green paint

* Quantity as needed or desired

in Chapter 3. Jeff then applied a thin layer of Durham's Water Putty to the rocks, giving them a smoother texture. After the putty dries, color the rocks with washes of acrylic or hobby paints. Lightweight foam castings from Scenic Express were also used some areas.

Follow the basic scenery methods shown in earlier chapters. The black paint used for the initial scenery base, **26**, better replicates the ground in coal country. The parking lot by the shanty was made with Woodland Scenics fine ballast and cinders.

Jeff scratchbuilt the coal loader, with the help of Radical Flats wall and roof panels from King Mill Enterprises. You can add more structures if you'd like.

Paint all exposed areas of the backdrop a flat sky blue color. If you prefer printed backdrops, see Chapters 2 and 3. Paint the exposed frame members with a semi-gloss deep green, **27**.

Mounting brackets

Cut members AA and BB for the wall brackets. Add hinges, **28**, which allow the brackets to fold to the wall. If you omit the hinges, lengthen members AA by ¾" so they can be glued and screwed to member BB. Install ¼" dowel pins or short lengths of ¼" dowels in the braces at the outer leg pockets, **29**. This keeps the brackets from moving while they are supporting the layout. If you don't add the leg pockets, simply drill 5⁄16" holes in frame members B for the dowels.

For the corner bracket, cut members U and V. Fasten members V to U with 1¼" drywall screws and glue, **30**.

34 One fellow at the camp appears to be considering a hop onto the passing boxcar.

35 One of many possible layout extension arrangements is a straight frame clamped perpendicular to the layout with a triangular piece added at the inside corner.

Mount the brackets so all three frames are level at the height you choose, **31**, **32**. Since the four wall brackets are designed with the dowel pins for the leg pockets, try to locate them at the leg pocket points of the straight frames. Some wall construction types and mounting methods may not permit you to locate the brackets at these points. If this is the case, install them as close as possible to the outer ends for maximum support, and add blocking to the frames as needed.

Setup and rolling stock

To keep the layout moveable, secure the layout sections to each other with clamps or bolts/nuts/washers. To set up the layout on the wall brackets, begin by setting one straight section in place. Clamp or otherwise fasten the corner section to it. Finish by fastening or clamping the other straight section to the corner piece.

If you plan to leave the layout on the brackets, you can simply fasten the sections together with screws.

Small locomotives and short rolling stock will of course look appropriate and perform best.

Variations

• Use the leg construction method shown in Chapter 3.

• Choose an N or HO track plan.

• Use the DC wiring shown in Chapter 2 if using one locomotive by yourself for switching.

• Use DC wiring with blocks and selector switches to run two locomotives. See Chapter 3 as well as Andy Sperandeo's book *Easy Model Railroad Wiring* (Kalmbach).

• Incorporate an automatic reversing circuit as shown in Chapter 6.

• Use fold-down shelf brackets—available from Rockler in the Suppliers and Manufacturers Section.

• Extend the layout with additional sections, **35**.

• To make an outside corner instead of the inside one demonstrated here, construct a square or triangular frame, or one with a convex curved front. No backdrop will be necessary.

1

This portable work station holds a vital selection of hobby tools and materials and can easily be stored between work sessions. When open, it stands by itself on a desk, table, or other work surface.

CHAPTER EIGHT

Compact work area

Building a desktop, fold-up work station

If you are having trouble finding space for a layout, you probably do not have much space for model building. One idea is to use part of a garage or workshop. However, garages can be unfriendly in extremes of weather. And workshops, speaking from experience, can get old when dirt and dust from the other workshop operation gives some undesired "weathering" to your models. In keeping with the theme of this book, this chapter shows you how to make a space-saving work station. Of course, you must have a location, such as a table or desk, where you can set it up. The negotiation with your family or housemates will obviously be your job. When it's not in use, you can fold up the work station in seconds, **2**, and store it in a very small space, **3**.

A self-healing cutting mat fits inside the work station when folded.

The work station is stored in a vanity.

Construction

The plans for the work station are shown in **4**. Begin by cutting the parts, **5**. Assemble each of the three basic box frames just as you did the layout frame in Chapter 5, using no. 8 x 1½" flathead wood screws. Glue the outside frame members of each box together, but omit the glue for the interior shelves. This will allow you to add or rearrange shelves later to make best use of the space available.

Fasten members A, B, and C together as shown to make the main box. Then assemble members E and D to form the two smaller boxes. Now place all three boxes face down and attach their plywood backs, **6**. Use no. 8 x 1" flathead wood screws for member F and no. 6 x ¾" flathead wood screws for member G.

Flip all the boxes over onto their backs. Fasten the shelf edges (members H and I) to shelves (members C and innermost members E), **7**. Use no. 6 x ¾" flathead wood screws for this task. Be sure to place members I where they will not strike members A when the box is closed; this is why they are slightly smaller than members E.

Install the four hinges on members A and D, **8**. Drill the appropriate size holes for the handle in top member B and fasten it with the screws included. Be sure to get a handle that has through-bolts instead of screws for strength.

The catches are the positive-closure type, which are used in vehicles like campers. You can buy them through Constantine's or The Woodworker's Store (see the list of suppliers and manufacturers in the appendix). Again, fasten them to top members B and E,

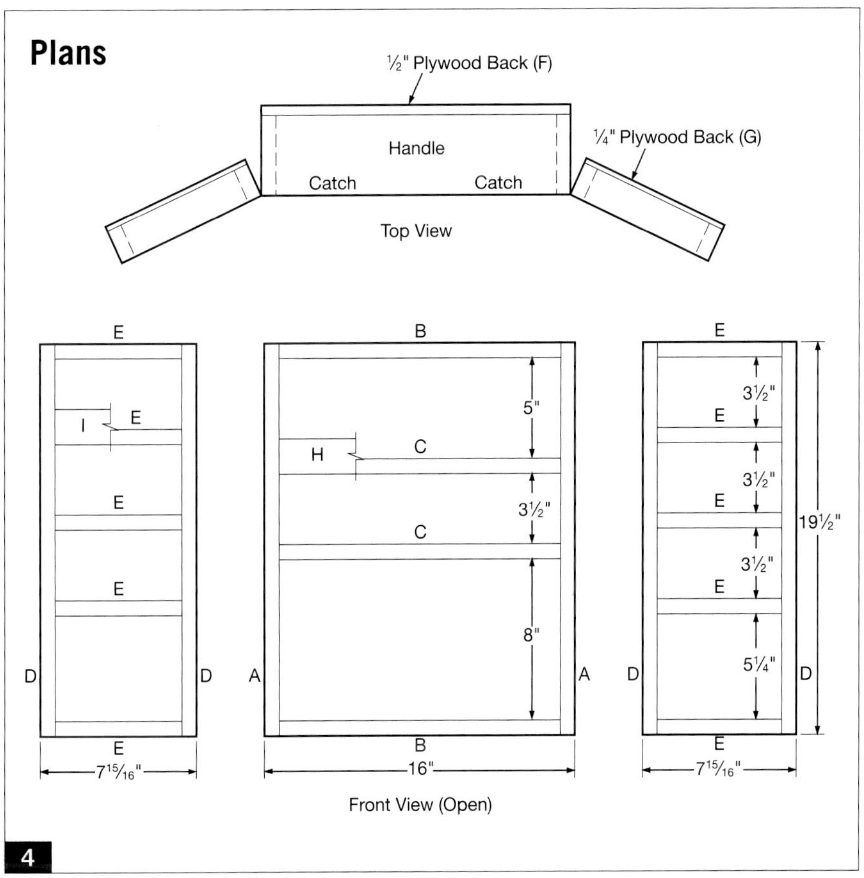

Cutting Diagrams

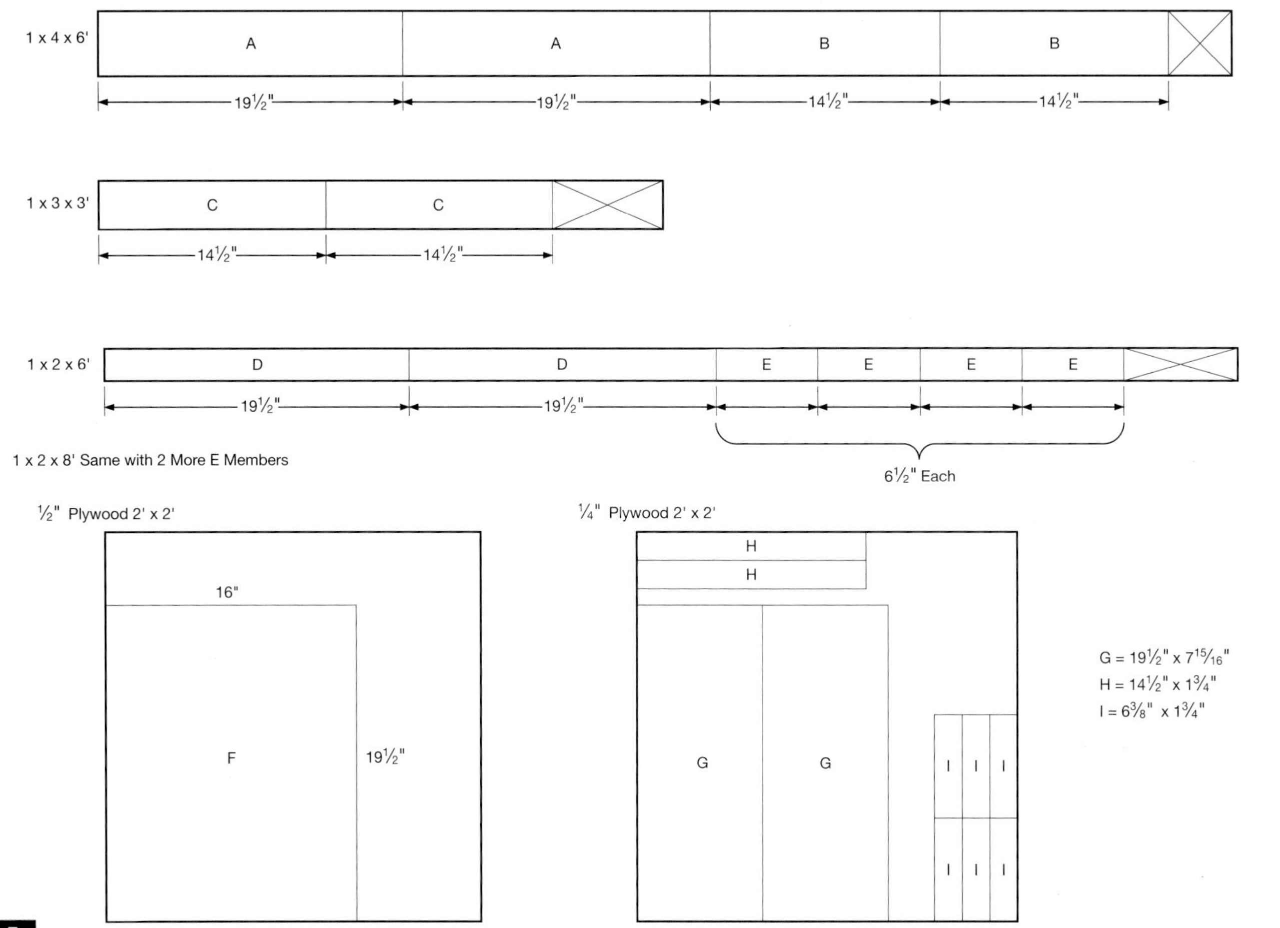

5

6

Assemble the box with flathead wood screws in similar fashion to the layout frames in earlier chapters.

7

Attach the shelf edges to their shelves with wood screws. Drill pilot holes to match the size of the screws used.

using the hardware that comes in their packages, **9**).

If you will be using this work station on a finished surface, glue felt to the bottoms of all three boxes. Buy the felt at an arts and crafts store, cut it to fit the bottom, and fasten it with wood glue, **10**. A self-healing cutting mat fits inside the station, and is a must for protecting your table or desk.

Variations

• Substitute pegboard in place of plywood for any of the backs, and use peg hardware and bins to arrange tools and materials.

• Build one or more shelves to swivel outward for easier access to tools and materials.

• Use clear acrylic instead of plywood for the shelf edges.

Fasten the hinges near each end of each side. The appropriate screws are provided with the hinges.

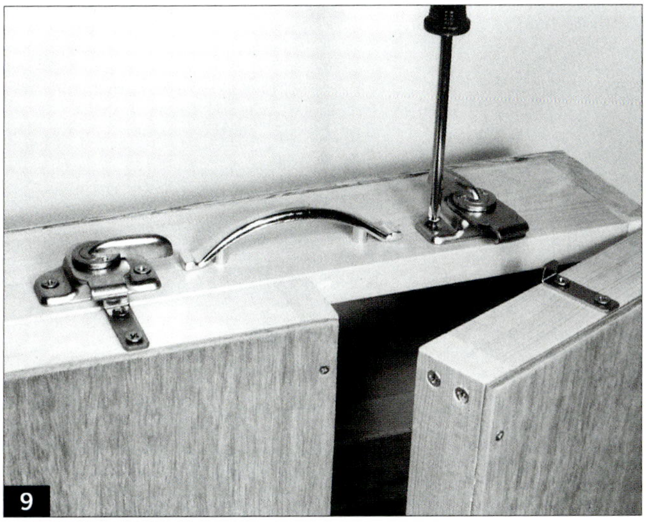

Attach the catches to the small doors first, then use screws to secure their mating sections onto the main box.

Spread glue evenly on the bottom of the box with a brush or your finger. Press the felt pieces firmly in place.

Bill of materials

Lumber
- 1 x 4, 6' white pine, 1
- 1 x 3, 3' white pine, 1
- 1 x 2, 6' white pine, 1
- 1 x 2, 8' white pine, 1
- ½" plywood, 2' x 2' sheet
- ¼" plywood, 2' x 2' sheet

Hardware
- Handle
- Hinges, 4
- Catches, 2
- * Wood screws, no. 8 x 1½" flathead
- * Wood screws, no. 8 x 1" flathead
- * Wood screws, no. 6 x ¾" flathead

Miscellaneous
- Felt, 12" x 18"
- * Wood glue
- * Tool holders of your choice

* Quantity as necessary or desired

Set up the work station at any convenient location. Be sure to protect against spills when painting or gluing.

1

CHAPTER NINE

Additional space-saving ideas

Tips and tricks you can use on many small layouts

Folding legs can save a great deal of space. One set of folding legs is in the open position showing the different parts: legs A, lower cross member B, upper cross member C, and hinge blocks D.

This chapter highlights some additional space-saving ideas that require a bit more advanced construction. They might appeal to those of you with more than basic woodworking skills, or they may simply generate an idea or two in your head as you plan and build your own small model railroad.

This is a close-up of the hinge and the anchor bolt and wing nut that holds upper cross member C to the layout frame.

When both wing nuts are removed, the leg pair swings in. The slot in cross member C accommodates the anchor bolt seen at left.

This shows how one set of legs (with longer cross members B and C) nests inside the other leg set. The red arrows show the holes in cross member B, which accommodate the anchor bolts and wing nuts on the layout frame.

With the legs in the folded position, the wing nuts can be added and secured to hold the legs in place.

Folding legs

These legs are used on two of my Ntrak modules, but could be useful for any portable layout, whether self-contained, modular, or sectional. They fold and store more quickly than the legs illustrated in Chapters 3 and 7.

The legs are made in pairs that nest inside each other when closed. When open, the legs are supported by a pair of wing nuts and anchor bolts, **1**. With the layout on its side, the bracket is released, **2**, and the pair of legs pivots on hinges that are mounted on a block under the scenery, **3**. One pair of legs nests inside the other in the stored position, **4**, and are held to the frame with another pair of hanger bolts and the same wing nuts, **5**. See Chapter 2 for a description of hanger bolt installation.

I cut some lumber down to size on a table saw to save weight, but this is not necessary. Here are the materials I used for leg assemblies, along with acceptable substitutes:

• Legs **A**: 1¼" square stock. Substitute: 2 x 2 boards

• Cross members **B** and **C**: ¼" x 1" stock. Substitute: 1 x 2 boards.

• Hinge block **D**: ¾" plywood. Substitute: any ¾" thick lumber

• Hinges: one pair of hinges for each set of legs

Before making the legs, plan which set of legs will nest into the other. Cut all members and make the anchor bolt slots in upper cross members C.

Make two sets of legs by mounting cross members B and C onto two legs A. The inner set, which folds closed first, must have longer cross members than the outer set, **4**. Mount the lower cross member B facing the inside of the layout and the top cross member C facing the outside—toward the frame end, **1**.

Place each set of legs into its upright position and fasten the hinges with the screws provided to both the legs and the blocks. Install anchor bolts

6

The layout cradle is supporting the left side of the layout from Chapter 3 as two legs support the right side. The author's son, Brian, is at the rolling stock storage box on the cradle shelf.

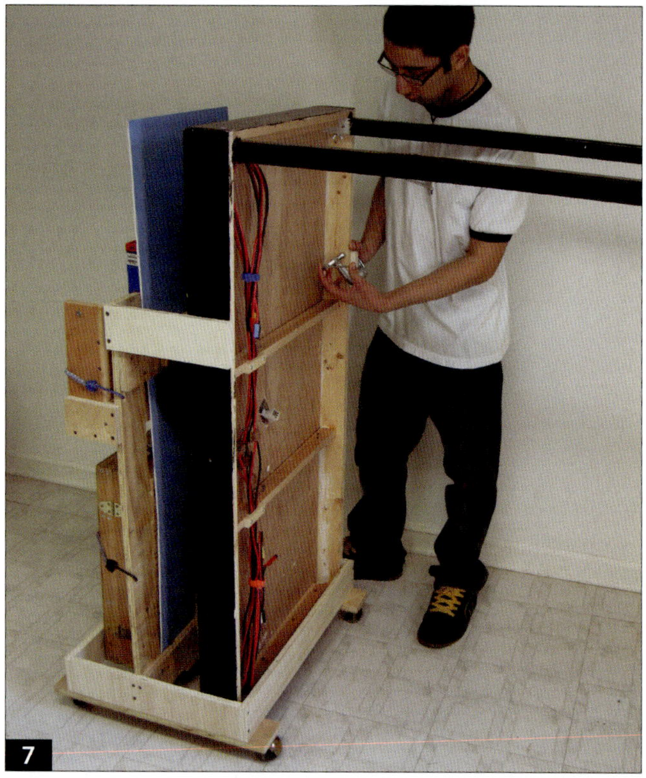

7

Brian clamps the layout upright in the cradle. He has moved the backdrop down into the center of the cradle and secured the control box to the shelf.

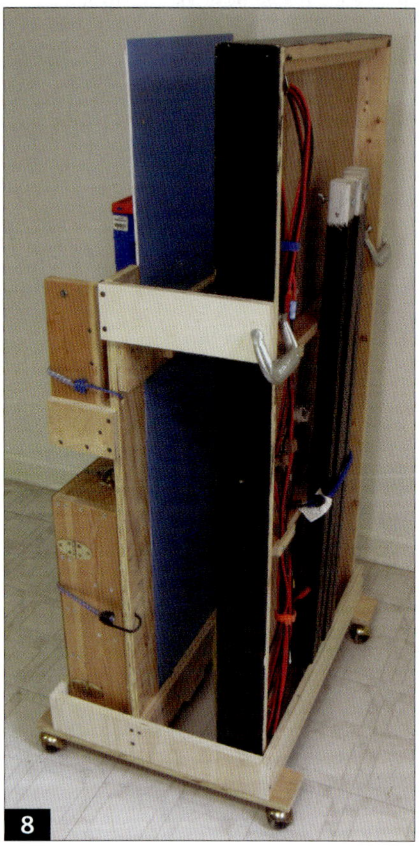

8

Everything is on the cradle and ready to be stowed away. The legs are secured to the bottom of the layout frame.

to the frame end to support the leg sets in the open position. Nest the legs and mount the anchor bolts to the frame to hold the sets in the closed position.

A folding bracket may be used to support the legs in the upright position instead of the anchor bolts and wing nuts in the frame ends. Various types of folding leg brackets and folding table supports are available in home centers such as Lowe's or from Constantine's or Rockler—see the appendix.

Rolling cradle

I designed a rolling cradle to easily carry one small layout upright, along with additional tools, rolling stock, or other materials, to a storage location. I built mine in a size to handle the layout from Chapter 3, but you could make it to accommodate different layouts or modules. Note that I temporarily fastened the removable section in place by driving screws in from the ends.

When the layout is used, one end is placed on the cradle and the other end on two legs, **6**. For storage, the layout is clamped upright into the cradle, **7**, the backdrop and legs are stowed, and away it goes (see photo 2 in the introduction). The opposite side of the cradle holds additional items such as the control box and rolling stock storage on the shelf and the work station from Chapter 8 on the bottom. The backdrop slips down in between members A. An elastic cord holds the legs to the layout frame, **8**.

The cradle utilizes all 1 x 4 boards. Alternatively, ¾" plywood could be cut into 3½"-wide strips for all members, as I have done. The list of members and their cut lengths is:

- A: 24¼"
- B: 36⅜" (this provides a layout height of 40" above the floor with the casters I used—adjust as necessary for layout leg height)
- C: 16½"
- D: approximately 25½" (cut to fit at respective construction step)
- E: 20¼"
- F: approximately 8¼" (cut to fit at respective construction step)
- G: 10½"
- H: 12"
- I: 24¼"
- J: 5"

Cradle plans

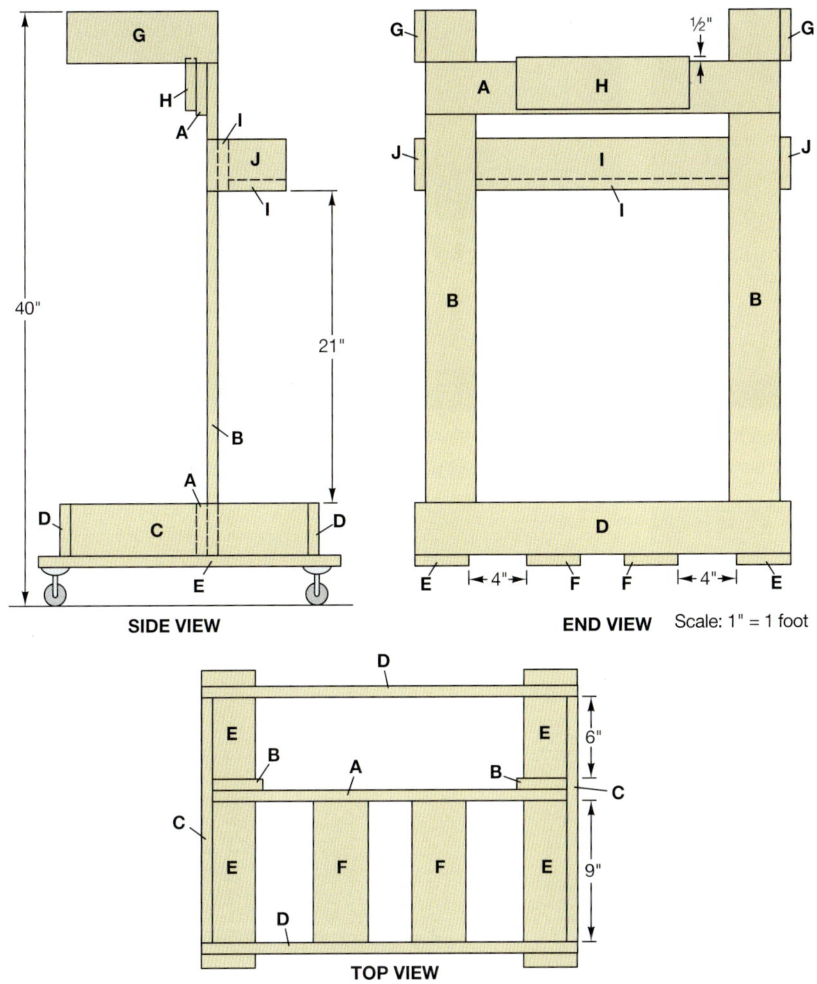

9

10

Here's the cradle itself after construction.

If you use 1 x 4s, you will need four 8-foot-long boards. Cut the following members from each:

- A, B, C, H
- A,B, C, J, J
- D, E, F, G, I
- D, E, F, G, I

If you use ¾" plywood instead, you will need a 4' x 4' sheet. Either way, remember four casters and the elastic cords to secure the items to be carried. Once all the members have been cut, construct the cradle according to **9** and **10** in the following sequence, using wood glue and 1¼" drywall screws:

- Fasten A members to B
- Fasten C members to A/B assembly
- Fasten D members to C
- Fasten E members to A/B/C/D assembly, overlapping equally on either side
- Fasten F members to A and D
- Fasten G members to B
- Fasten H member to upper A member, leaving enough clearance for anything inside the layout frame. It may be necessary to shim this out with some cardboard so the layout end fits.
- Fasten members I to each other
- Fasten I/I shelf assembly to members B
- Fasten shelf ends J to B and I
- Install casters

With a bit of redesign, the cradle could be sized to handle a pair of layout modules or sections. Make the dimension on the storage side the same as the layout side and extend members F. To use the cradle to set up a mating pair of modules or section, modify the top of the cradle to allow the layout frames ends to butt against each other.

Bar layout

This layout was featured in the first edition of this book. It requires more advanced tools and construction techniques than the layouts featured in this edition. Although a bar is a less-common piece of furniture in a typical home, this layout contains some features that you may find useful.

This layout's history yields some insights. Being the first layout I built into a piece of furniture (in this case, an existing bar, **11**, it took no additional room from the house. I made the top with ½"-thick glass in a wood frame, but I originally omitted the hinges. This required me to move that heavy beast every time I needed access to the layout. After quickly learning that I was too optimistic, I added hinges to the top. It is held open by two removable wood support brackets with pins in each end, **12**.

The layout's size is approximately 2 x 5 feet. This allows for a relatively

Family and friends enjoy the bar-top layout. Since the layout was added to an existing piece of furniture, it took up no additional space.

When open, the glass top is supported by brackets. The bracket in the foreground, shows the pins in each end that hold it in place.

This layout has some hidden track that requires access. A scenery lift-out section (right) covers the opening—a technique that can be used on a layout of any size.

The rear of the layout shows (left to right) a lowered section, the control panel, and the power pack. The lowered section contains the river below the wood trestle visible in the photo at left.

interesting track plan—a "folded dog-bone"—with one end loop on top of the other. A passing siding and a number of spurs facing in both directions allow for switching in addition to continuous running.

The scenery includes two lift-out sections that are removed to access lower levels of track, **13**, where the loops are stacked on top of one another. Before refining the rock technique shown in Chapter 3, I used rock molds on this layout with success. Otherwise, the scenery techniques for this layout are similar to those presented in other chapters of this book.

I named all buildings after friends and family members. Included are some inside jokes that have proven to be interesting—for example, the burned-down shed across the street from the firehouse named after a friend who is a fire chief.

Looking at the back of the layout, **14**, other features are apparent. The lowered sections allow the scenery to extend vertically down below the basic layout box. Another feature is the small custom-made control panel. The momentary push button switches control the turnouts, and the toggle switches turn electric blocks on and off.

End table layout

Another end table? Yes, but one with very different features than the one in Chapter 5. Like the bar, it requires advanced tools and techniques, but you may want to incorporate versions of its features in your project, **15**.

The 15½" x 21" layout is visible from the top and all four sides through an acrylic panel that is built into the top and a four-sided acrylic box that surrounds the layout. The layout/acrylic box assembly slides into the table from either side, **16**. The layout's bridges and buildings are under construction, but in the meantime the layout can be displayed. The design makes it is easy to remove the layout to perform work while not affecting the use of the table. Another acrylic panel rests on steel rods for the lower shelf.

15

Here's the end table with the layout in place.

16

Sliding the layout out for operating access or to work on this layout, which is still being detailed, is easy. You can see the layout itself fits inside a four-sided acrylic box. Under both the layout and the acrylic is a sheet of hardboard.

17

The power pack fits nicely in a drawer under the layout. It stays hidden when the layout is not operating.

18

Here are the wire connectors in the rear of the layout. This close-up view shows the double layer of Homosote supporting the layout, as well as the hardboard sheet under the acrylic.

The power pack is in a small drawer, **17**. All wiring runs through a hole in the drawer bottom. Two pairs of wires—to feed track and accessories — run to removable connectors accessible through the back of the acrylic box, **18**. The track plan is a simple oval with small-radius curves and two dummy sidings. When finished, it will be a selectively compressed version of my hometown and the shortline railroad that served it.

The tapered legs and the beveled top edges are modern touches that I incorporated to coordinate the end table with existing furniture in the same room. A table saw made these features within my reach. However, there is no reason why you could not modify the coffee table concept in Chapter 4 to accommodate a slide-in, acrylic-sided layout such as this, in either coffee table size or end table size. Chapter 6 illustrates the methods for cementing acrylic panels.

One final idea is to purchase a shadow-box style table, such as the one shown back in Chapter 4 **(4- 22)**. Then you can add an acrylic-sided layout such as the one shown here.

SUPPLIERS AND MANUFACTURERS

Allposters.com
(Photo posters for backdrops)
888-654-0143
www.allposters.com

Atlas Model Railroad Co.
(Track, accessories, locomotives, rolling stock, structures, books)
378 Florence Ave.
Hillside, NJ 07205
908-687-0880
www.atlasrr.com

Bachmann
(Track, accessories, structures)
1400 E. Erie St.
Philadelphia, PA 19124
www.bachmanntrains.com

Circuitron
(Electronics supplies)
211 RocBaar Dr.
Romeoville, IL 60446-1163
815-886-9010
www.circuitron.com

Constantine's Wood Center
(Woodworking tools, hardware, and finishing products)
1040 E. Oakland Park Blvd.
Ft. Lauderdale, FL 33334
954-561-1716
www.constantines.com

Digitrax
(Digital Command Control equipment)
2443 Transmitter Rd.
Panama City, FL 32404-3157
850-872-9890
www.digitrax.com

Kalmbach Publishing Co.
(Model railroading books)
21027 Crossroads Circle
Waukesha, WI 53187-0986
1-800-533-6644
www.kalmbach.com

King Mill Enterprises
(Radical Flats photo background buildings)
434-962-2514
www.kingmill.com

Micro-Mark
(Modeling tools and supplies)
340 Snyder Ave.
Berkeley Heights NJ 07922-1595
1-800-225-1066
www.micromark.com

Midwest Products Co., Inc.
(Cork roadbed and other supplies)
400 S. Indiana St.
P.O. Box 564
Hobart, IN 46342
800-348-3497
www.midwestproducts.com

National Model Railroad Association (NMRA)
4121 Cromwell Rd.
Chattanooga TN 37421
423-892-2846
www.nmra.org

Ntrak Publishing
(Ntrak standards, newsletter, N scale information)
1150 Wine Country Pl.
Templeton CA 93465
805-434-5058
www.ntrak.org

Piedmont Plastics, Inc.
(Acrylic panels and accessories)
9000 Virginia Manor Road
Beltsville, MD 20705-4216
301-881-7900
www.piedmontplastics.com

Realistic Backgrounds
(Photo backdrops)
P.O. Box 211
Presto, PA 15142
412-276-7746
www.realisticbackgrounds.com

Rockler Woodworking and Hardware
(Woodworking tools, hardware, and finishing products)
4365 Willow Dr.
Medina, MN 55340
800-279-4441
www.rockler.com

Scenic Express
(Scale Concrete and other scenery materials)
175 Sheffield Dr., #100
Delmont, PA 15626
800-234-9995

The Shelf Layouts Company, Inc.
(Custom model railroads and layout design by Lance Mindheim)
3204 Verona Dr.
Silver Spring, MD 20906
301-404-8164
www.shelflayouts.com

Waddell Manufacturing Company
(Table legs)
1676 Commerce Dr.
Stow, OH 44224
800-433-1737
www.waddellmfg.com

Wm. K. Walthers
(Model railroad distributor and manufacturer)
P.O. Box 3039
Milwaukee, WI 53201-3039
800-487-2467
www.walthers.com

Woodcraft Supply, LLC
(Woodworking tools, hardware, and finishing products)
1177 Rosemar Rd.
P.O. Box 1686
Parkersburg, WV 26102
1-800-225-1153
www.woodcraft.com

Woodland Scenics
(Scenery materials and details)
P.O. Box 98
Linn Creek, MO 65052
573-346-5555
www.woodlandscenics.com

Mat Chibbaro is a fire protection engineer with the OSHA National Office, a part-time fire protection lecturer at the University of Maryland, and a life member of the College Park, Md., Volunteer Fire Department. His interest in model railroading began in Milltown, N.J., through which ran the Raritan River Railroad. Perhaps the short trains that ran on this short line cultivated his interest in small railroads. For the last 15 years, most of his model railroad time has been with the Northern Virginia Ntrak club. Mat lives in Maryland with his wife, Erna, son, Brian, and daughter, Stephanie.

— ACKNOWLEDGEMENTS —

First, thanks to my family (Erna, Brian, and Stephanie) for their patience, understanding, and support of my hobby, which has provided many hours of enjoyment for the whole family. I also appreciate their support during the preparation of this book, especially the frequent calls for assistance—either to take pictures or model for them.

I appreciate the assistance provided to me in various forms by my fellow modelers, primarily Jeff Peck, the modeler responsible for the layout in Chapter 7.

Final recognition goes to the companies that donated materials for this book: Atlas Model Railroad Company, Bachmann, Digitrax, King Mill Enterprises, Lowe's, and Woodland Scenics.

—Mat Chibbaro

MUST-HAVE BOOKS FOR EVERY MODELER

Realistic Layouts: Use the Art of Illusion to Model Like a Pro

Capture the feeling of the real world in miniature! This book will help you refine many areas of your layout, covering topics such as scenic elements, structures and the aesthetic of the overall environment.

#12828 • $21.99

Multideck Design for Model Railroads

Discover the many methods for designing and building a multideck layout along with all the tried-and-true tips Tony Koester has gathered along the way. This go-to book includes many examples on lighting, construction, operation, and other facets of two- and three-deck layouts.

#12837 • $21.99

Workshop Tips & Projects for Model Railroaders

A compilation of insider tips and projects from *Model Railroader*, covering tools, painting and decaling, weathering, track and wiring, structures, scenery, locomotives, and freight cars in a friendly, knowledgeable style.

#12475 • $19.99

Building the Right-Sized Layout

Get the perfect book to help with planning a room-sized layout for your home. This book from Thomas Klimoski features 5 track plans covering details on how to create a manageable layout with space, time, and resources in mind.

#12825 • $21.99

Kalmbach Media

Buy now from your local hobby shop!

Shop at KalmbachHobbyStore.com